Pretty Guardian ★

Sailor Moon

2

Pretty Guardian
Sailor Moon
Act 7
Mammoru Chiba, Tuxedo Mask

CONTENTS

ACT 7 MAMORU CHIBA, TUXEDO MASK...3

ACT 8 MINAKO, SAILOR V…49

ACT 9 SERENITY, PRINCESS…81

ACT 10 MOON…122

ACT 11 REUNION, ENDYMION…164

Pretty Guardian SAILOR MOON

So you're awake?

Mamoru... Chiba?
Why is he... here?!
This place... Is it...
You're in...
...my room.

Mamoru Chiba's room?
Why would I be in his room...?
AH!!
Do you remember?
B-BMP
You passed out, and absolutely nothing could wake you up.

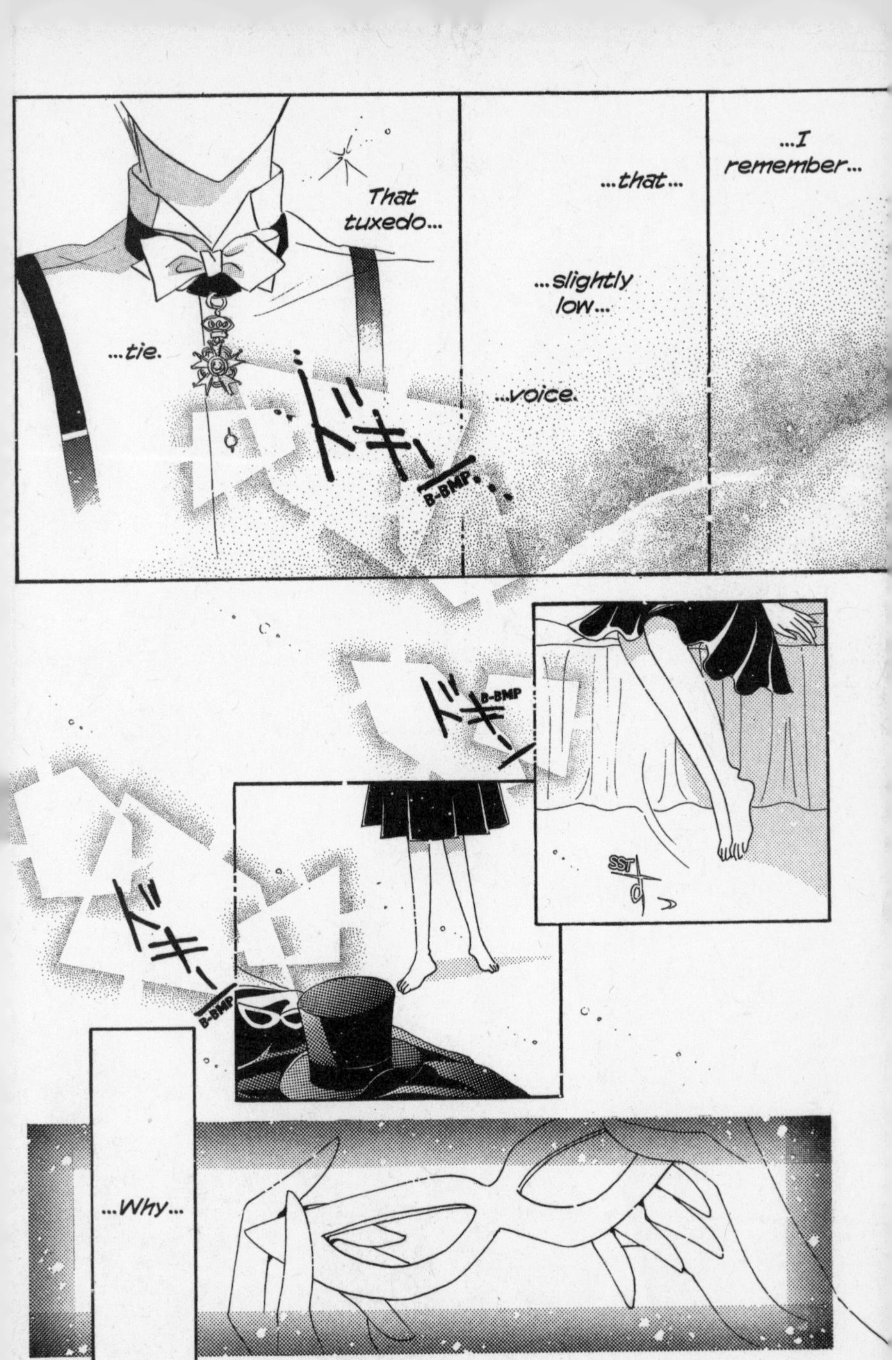
...I remember...
...that...
...slightly low...
...voice.
That tuxedo...
...tie.
ドキ
B-BMP
ドキー
B-BMP
SST
ドキー
B-BMP
...Why...

...didn't I notice before...?
The color of those eyes, like I could be sucked in...
...Tuxedo Mask...?

Why...?
Why are you... Tuxedo Mask...?
B-BMP
ドキン
It...
It's for my memory.
That's why I have to get my hands on the "Legendary Silver Crystal."
Your memory?

"Ah ha ha!"
"Come on, Dad! Mom! I wanna go for a drive now!"
"It's such a shame about that couple..."
"But the fact that their son, Mamoru, lived through it is a miracle."
"On the other hand..."
Who... am I...?
Why am I here?
I can't remember! Who am I?!

I lost my parents in an accident on my sixth birthday.
...and at the same time, I lost my memory.

"Your name is Mamoru Chiba."
That's what they told me at the hospital... but I still don't remember it for myself.
Am I actually Mamoru Chiba? Or...
...am I somebody else? For years I had no idea.

And I started having the same dream over and over.

"Find the 'Legendary Silver Crystal'... Please..."

"Legendary Silver Crystal"... Just that phrase.

Time and time again in my dreams...

And before I knew it...
...I was stealing through the city at night like some strange sleep-walker!
Wearing a tuxedo like some phantom thief.
The only clue to my past memories...
...are the words, "Find the 'Legendary Silver Crystal.'"
ドキン..
B-BMP

...What about you?
Eh?
ドキッ B-BMP
You're looking for it too, right?
The "Legendary Silver Crystal."
... Why?
Um... I...
... Well it isn't...
...どきん B-BMP
...quite so... well de-fined...
Luna told me to find it and protect it, so...
...どきん B-BMP
B-BMP ...どきん
...I see.
B-BMP ...どきん
I never dreamed...
...that he'd...
...have a reason like that...

"I never wanted to believe that Tuxedo Mask could be an enemy, but..."
"The 'Legendary Silver Crystal' is something we must never allow to fall into enemy hands!"
ドキ B-BMP
...Luna is sounding an alarm inside my head.
But it's already...
...too late.
Our secrets...
...are now revealed to each other.
Is it really so wrong to trust him?
... Luna!
ドキ B-BMP
What'll should I do...?
My heart is racing...
...I feel...
ドキ B-BMP
Right now...

...that if time stopped at this moment...
...it would be...
...just fine by me.
ドキ…!
BA-BUMP
...Luna is waiting. I...
...have to...go home...

Usako...
BA-BUMP

...Usako.
Your bag...
...He called me...
..."Usako"...
That's what he said.
...Since he's "Mamoru"...
...I could call him "Mamo-chan"...
...maybe?
ドキ
ドキ
シャフッ
I brought it with me...
...his broken pocket watch...
And soon...
...the curtain of night...
Second Year, Class One, Usagi Tsukino

...will fall...
CROWN GAME CENTER
CROWN
It's true.
They've all awakened a bit...
...but the memories of their time as guardians...
They don't remember that.
Especially Sailor Moon. She's still not there yet as a guardian.
It's too soon. We should wait longer.

But we don't have time, Luna.
The enemy will be upon us soon.
Innocent people are in danger.

...

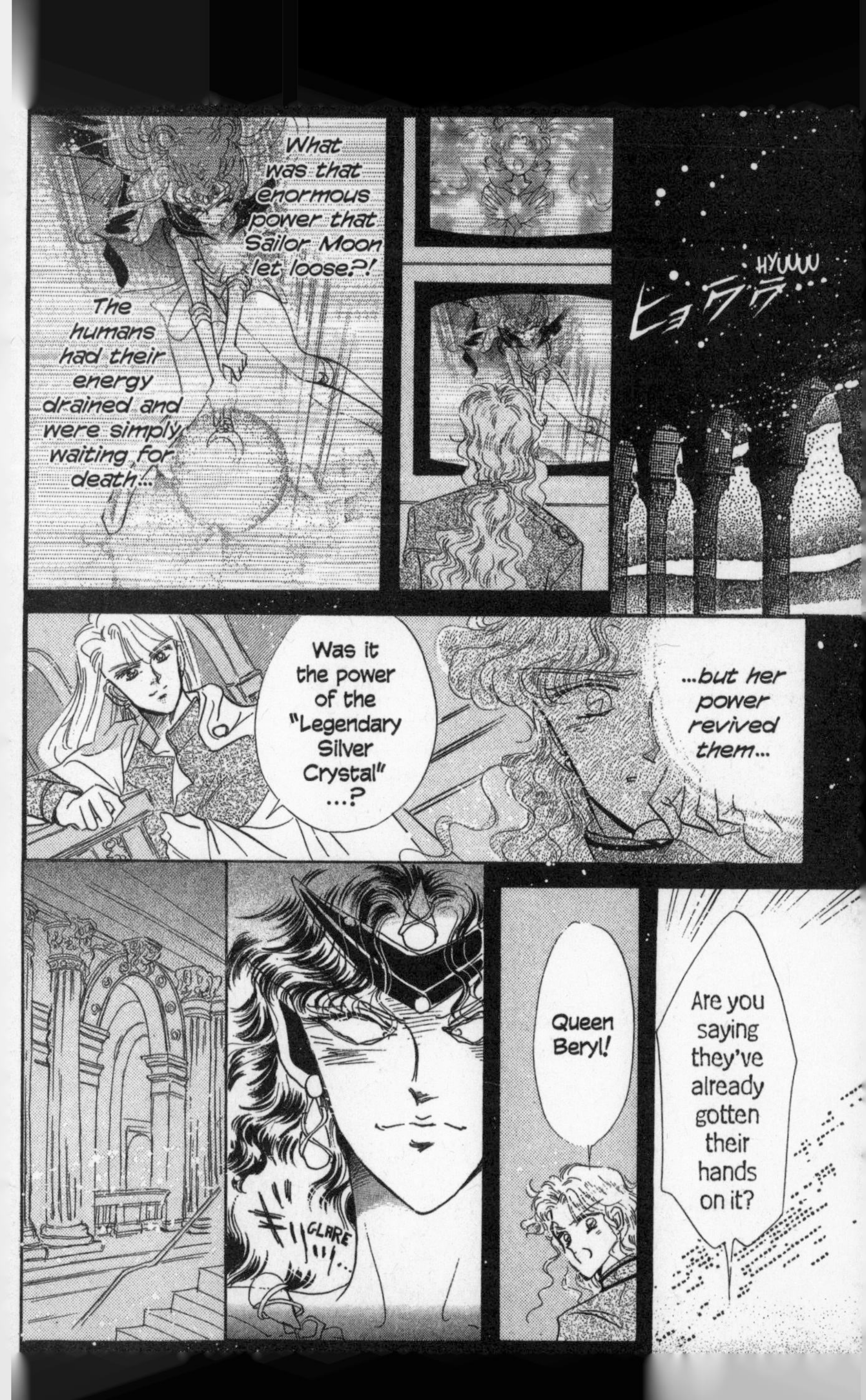
HYUUU
ヒョウウ
What was that enormous power that Sailor Moon let loose?!
The humans had their energy drained and were simply waiting for death...
...but her power revived them...
Was it the power of the "Legendary Silver Crystal" ...?
Are you saying they've already gotten their hands on it?
Queen Beryl!
GLARE

ピチャン
PLUNK
ギイイイ
KREEEEE
Our great ruler...
Queen Metalia!
I call on you to awaken!
I offer glorious energy to
revive you for a short while!

Oooh...
SHUUUU
...Hurry...
Hurry! Obtain the "Legendary Silver Crystal"...! And offer it up to me...! I desire energy...! Ohhh...
Queen Metalia!
I am using my minions, the Four Kings of Heaven to search the world over.
But no clue has arisen.
All that is left is the land of Japan.

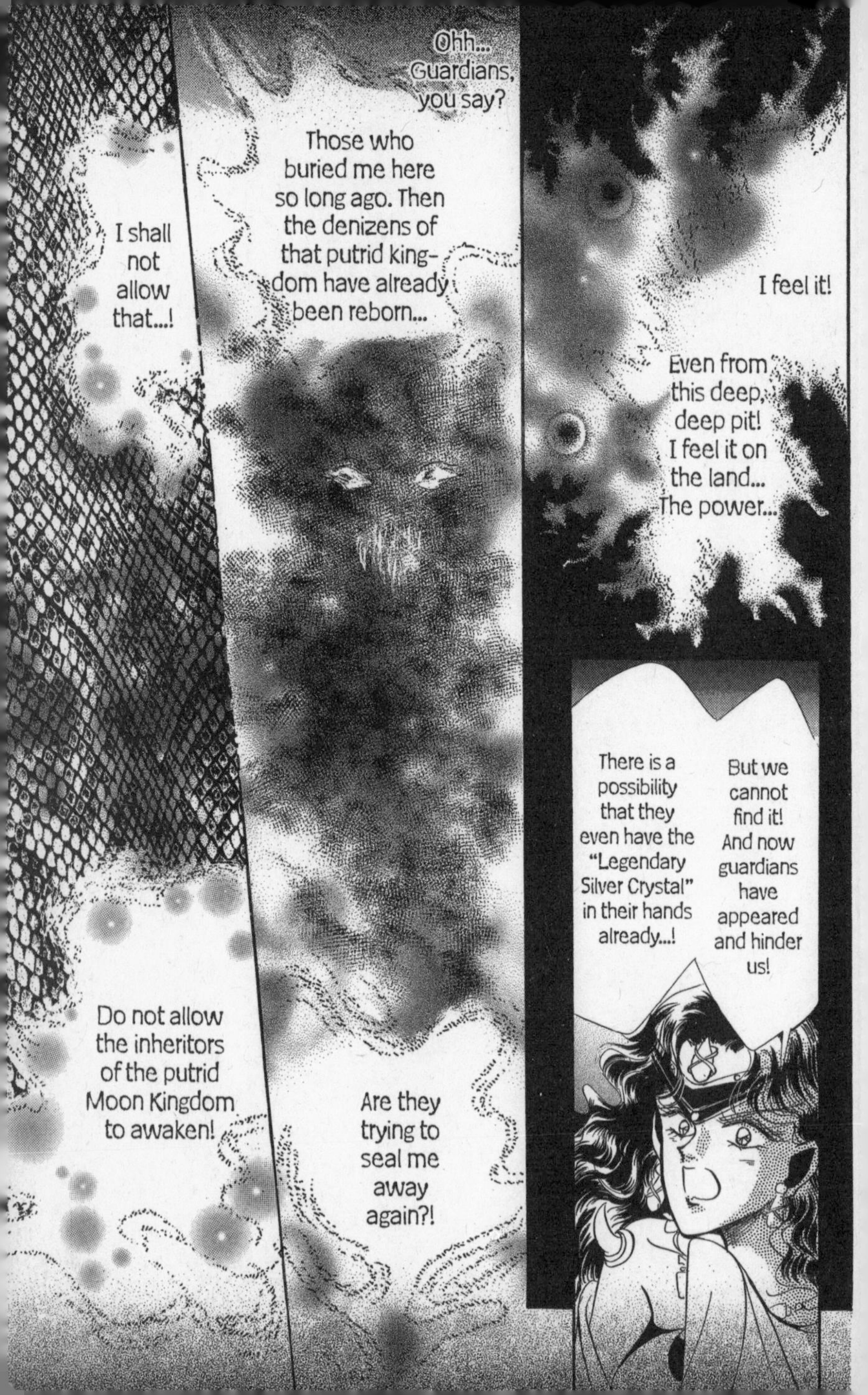
I feel it!
Even from this deep, deep pit! I feel it on the land... The power...
But we cannot find it! And now guardians have appeared and hinder us!
There is a possibility that they even have the "Legendary Silver Crystal" in their hands already...!
Ohh... Guardians, you say?
Those who buried me here so long ago. Then the denizens of that putrid king-dom have already been reborn...
Are they trying to seal me away again?!
I shall not allow that...!
Do not allow the inheritors of the putrid Moon Kingdom to awaken!

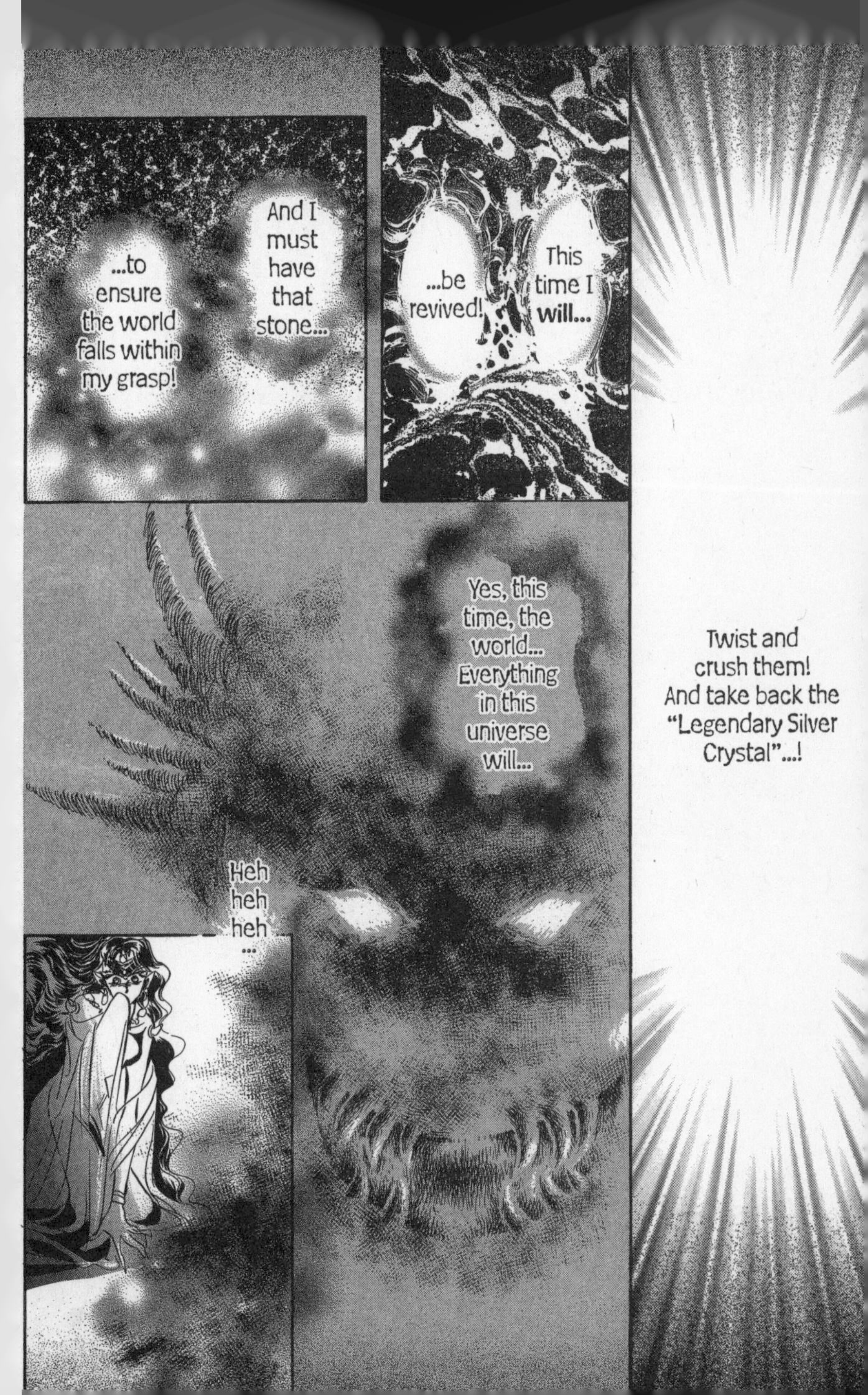
Twist and crush them! And take back the "Legendary Silver Crystal"...!
This time I will...
...be revived!
And I must have that stone...
...to ensure the world falls within my grasp!
Yes, this time, the world... Everything in this universe will...
Heh heh heh ...

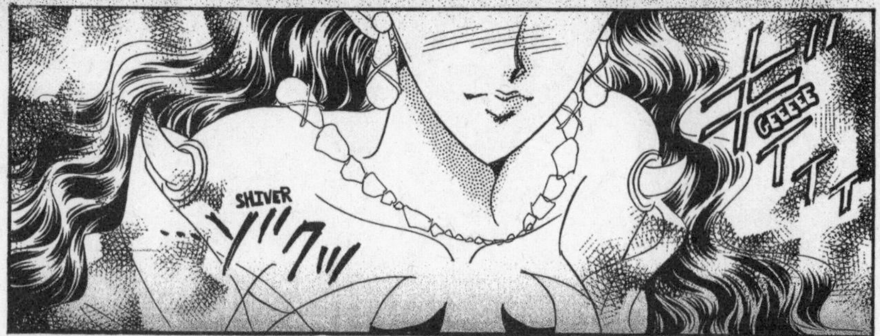
GEEEEE
SHIVER

As I watch, she grows darker and more expansive...

If I can truly revive Queen Metalia...
...she may eat this entire planet alive.

But there is no turning back.
From the moment I broke that seal...

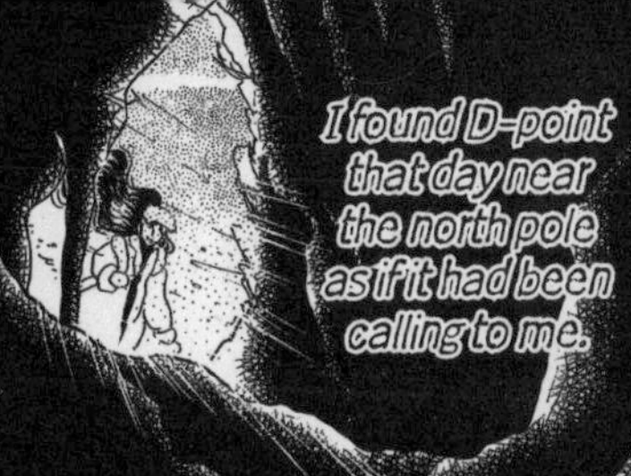
I found D-point that day near the north pole as if it had been calling to me.
That hidden, cursed ruined building...

It was the Dark Kingdom.
And, irresistibly drawn to it, I broke the seal...

Again, with my own hands, I freed Queen Metalia...
It was destiny!
The "Legendary Silver Crystal"...

It is my life's desire!
With it, this world is mine for the taking!!

Before Queen Metalia gets it, I must!! I must, if I am to make this planet my own!
HEH HEH...
Inheritors of the Moon Kingdom...?
Zoisite!
That one... That "Sailor Moon" perhaps knows who the holder of the "Legendary Silver Crystal" is. Or even...
...she may be hiding it herself!
VEEEN
Ah! Yumiko! Kuri! ♡

Yumiko
Kuri
Oh, you too, Naru-chan? You came to rent a video?

Lately Usagi hasn't had any time at all! SNIFF
So I thought I'd fill the weekend up watching videos.
Usagi, next time we meet, you'd better treat me to something tasty! ☆

So when did this huge video rental shop get built?

It's a chain, and they're springing up all over town!

And you're guaranteed to be able to rent the video you want, so everybody's coming here.

RENTAL SHOP DARK
BRANCH #2
RENTAL SHOP DARK
BRANCH #13
Did you see that new video?
Of course! Lately I've been totally absorbed in videos! I've pulled so many all-nighters, I'm wiped out!
You know the "Legendary Silver Crystal?"
AH!

They're saying that Sailor Moon has it hidden somewhere.
Sailor Moon ...?
ぶつぶつ MUMBLE MUMBLE...
24
DARK
ヴィ VEEEEN ン...
Rental Shop Dark...
I sense evil...
DINNG DONNG
キンコーン...
Lunch time! Lunch time! ♡
So what's in Mako-chan's lunch box today?
Heh heh! ♡ Today, I brought fruit sandwiches.
I recommend the strawberry one! ♡
Data on Sailor V?
Right. You said you were wondering about her, right? So I did a bit of investigating.
LA-LA! るんっ
YAAAY!
MUNCH MUNCH もぐもぐ
KLIKK カチャ
KLIKK カチャ

Sailor V
Name, Age: Yet to be ascertained.
Personal Identifying Info: Yet to be ascertained.
ID Number: Yet to be ascertained.
Address: Yet to be ascertained.
Work History: Yet to be ascertained.
Criminal Record: Yet to be ascertained.
Items Warranting Special Mention
-- Self-described "Champion of Justice"
-- In action, mainly in Tokyo area since 199X
-- Witness reports climbing into the hundreds
-- Sudden decrease in witness reports since Sailor Moon first appeared.
The phantom champion of justice...
... Sailor V...?
Say...
This crescent mark here that V-chan is wearing...
Don't you think it may have something to do with this Moon Kingdom that Luna was talking about?

Does it really bother you that much?
Luna said that she didn't feel anything from Sailor V...
May-be...
...it's that *you* feel something from V-chan through your own powers, Usagi-chan...
Remember what Luna said? We haven't fully awakened yet, right?
But Usagi-chan, you may be awakening little by little.
The healing effect from that stick Luna gave you focused a very strong power.
And we may all be guardians, but you, Usagi-chan, are our leader.
It is within the realm of possibility that you have a special power we do not possess.
Very strong power?
I have a special power...?

I think that was why I was able to release the power.

Besides, at the time, I had Tuxedo Mask there to support me.

But what saved everybody was the power in the moon stick!

I have to talk to everybody about that, huh?

Also...
...the fact that he knows that I'm Sailor Moon.
It's wrong for me to keep such a vital piece of information a secret, huh?

About Tuxedo Mask...
...and who he is.

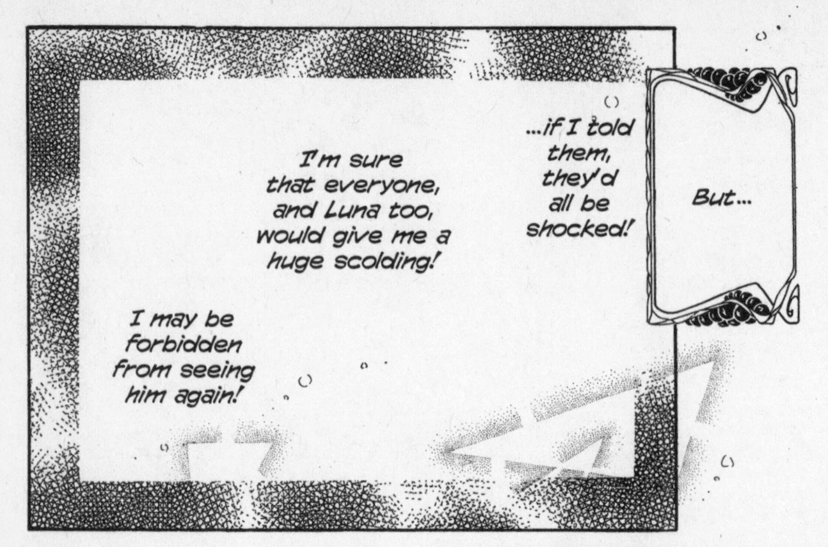
But...
...if I told them, they'd all be shocked!
I'm sure that everyone, and Luna too, would give me a huge scolding!
I may be forbidden from seeing him again!

Whenever I think of him... I don't know why, but...
...my chest feels so tight, it's hard to breathe.
I need to...
...keep it secret...
...just a little bit longer...

Hey, everyone! Look at all of you! In a place like this!
SHFF
I was wondering what you all were doing here.
The Sailor V game?
Umino ...
Sailor V data? You're kidding!
FLIP
FLIP
Who needs Sailor V these days? Now's when we should be investigating Sailor Moon, right, Usagi-chan?
Eh?!
GAK
I'm going to find her before anybody else does!
I'm going to be the first person to meet Sailor Moon face-to-face!
HEH HEH
Ah, Th-That scared me!
So he hasn't found me out yet, right?
HAHH HAHH
はあ はあ
D-Don't you think Umino's acting a little strange?
S-Scary!
B-BMP B-BMP
ドキドキ
MUMBLE MUMBLE
...ブツブツ

What's with him? He's unusually aggressive, huh?
Luna!
Umino had a weird look in his eyes, and he was babbling on and on...

Luna, it's been a long time since I've seen you come to school.
True. I've been holed up in the underground command center...
Hm? Where's Naru-chan? Don't you always have lunch with her?
Naru-chan...
...let's have lunch together...
MUMBLE MUMBLE
2-1
CHATTER CHATTER

Azabu Juban Shopping District

Ah!
Furu-chan!
Yo, Usagi-chan! Ami-chan!
The game center is dead these days. Not a single customer will come in!
I'm sure it's competition from all those video rental shops. Everybody's renting videos like crazy!
I don't watch them myself, but...
Videos...?
CRO W
MEOW! MEOW!
Usagi-chan, hurry up! Hurry!
Insert the video into the V-chan game here!
Into a game machine?!
This machine is directly connect-ed to the command center down below!
GACHIK
SAILOR V GAME START
Ehh?!
Is that right?!
BZZT
BZZT
KYAAA!

SHPOON
BZZT
BZZT
The video just came flying out! It's almost like the game machine re-jected it!
PAFF
This is no ordinary video! Maybe the work of the enemy?!
But Luna, what I want to know is what's with this V-chan game?!
Didn't that video break the machine?!
PEEP
ZZT ZZT
VAPP
What are you waiting for, Sailor Moon?!
It's a brain-washing video sent by the enemy, and the town's flooded with them!
And it isn't just brain-washing! The lives of the people are in danger!

Sailor V?!
V-chan in the game just talked to me?!
FFT
You're kidding ...!
Oh...!
Usagi-chan! Go!! I'll go down to the underground command center!
SHAA
!!
SHAA
This tape is using subliminals?!
Find Sailor Moon!
Grab Sailor Moon! She holds the secret to the "Legendary Silver Crystal"!
She must be captured alive!
Offer Sailor Moon up to the Dark Kingdom!!

SHUU
...What's this?! It's sucking out energy!!
?!

はあ
HAHH
It said the "Dark Kingdom" ?!

SHKK
SHKK
Find Sailor Moon!

Luna, what is that?!
They're using people like puppets one after another...
Who are they?! What are they after?!

Find her!
Where is she?! Where?!
Right here!

Pretty Guardian of Love and Justice in a Sailor Suit! Sailor Moon has arrived !!
Moon Healing Escalation!!
PAAAA
Huh ?!
Ah!
☆
CHATTER

Sailor Moon! So you came!!
SWISH
Trying to control people's minds while they are trying to enjoy their R&R time is unforgivable!
And in the name of the moon, I, Sailor Moon will now punish you!
Moon Twilight Flash!

!!
He vanished ?!
HYOOM
KYAA!!
GRABB
Now, tell me! Where is the "Legendary Silver Crystal" ?!
I don't know!
PCH
PCH
KRIK
Eyaaaah!
Evil spirit...
BWOOCGH
GWOOCH
...be exor-cized!!

I'll help out too, Rei!
Supreme Thunder!!
BWAAAN
BASHUU
Rei?! Mako?!
Unh ...
Humph! Little meddlers!

I can't take it anymore...
Tuxedo Mask...
GRRN GRRN ぐぐ
KRIKK
Save me...
GRIMMMP ぎゅうう....
There's a barrier in the way! I can't get close...
Kh...!
Die!
BWAAN
Usako...!!
EYAAAH!

KRAKK
HYUUM
KRUMBL
ボロッ
STCH
Sailor Moon, now! Get down!
SHANN
VSHAAA
URKK

...Who is she?!

That silhouette!
Could it be... But it can't...
Still I could tell...
...for a split second...
...like an electric shock going through my entire body!
...The phantom...
...champion of justice...
...Sailor V?!

Act 8
Minako, Sailor V

Pretty Guardian ★ Sailor Moon

Sailor. team.

Sailor V?!
Is she a fifth guardian?
No! It couldn't be! She's...
Sailor V?! The phantom champion of jus-tice...?
You're kidding! Why would she be here?!
She isn't like the Sailor V we've heard about...! The cos-tume she's wearing...
Luna ...!
--!
...くすっ
HEH

SST
That's true. I've hardly ever taken off this mask in front of other people.
Red goggles?! V-chan?!
For pity's sake! How rude can you get?!
Yes, she may be Sailor V, but...
...Her Highness is also...
...of the Kingdom of the Moon, Silver Millennium...
...and the blessed successor to the sacred royal treasure, the "Legendary Silver Crystal!"

She is Princess Serenity!
Sailor V is the princess?!
I knew it...!
Yes, V-chan has that mark on her forehead!

GLEEM
GLEEM
That has to be Princess Serenity's...
...mark...
SHMMM
What?!
My fore-head...
...feels hot...
PAASH
Princess Serenity...?!
My tiara...
...just trans-formed...
I get the feeling I...
...was just on the verge of remembering something very important...

AH
Who?! Who's watching us?!
WHOOSH
PASSH
FWOOSH
That man...!!

Princess Serenity...
...Hmm? That name...
...I get the feeling I've heard it somewhere before...
"Save me... Eyaaah!"
Usako...
HAAH
...はあっ

I wasn't strong enough...
...to protect her...
You've done a very good job so far, Sailor Moon.

...V-chan, who I've always admired, is right here in front of me!
And she's the princess!
It's like a dream!
I've been monitoring your progress through the game machine all this time...
...so to me, it doesn't feel like the first time we've met.
HEH HEH
The Sailor V game has been teaching you to fight through simulation, you know.
And it was effective.
She taught me how to fight through the V-chan game?
And when she talked to us, that was V-chan herself, huh?
SST

It's a pleasure to meet you, Sailor Jupiter.
VZZT
... Mars...
GRIMP
VZZT
...Just now...
For just an instant...
...I thought I saw some-thing...
I hope...
...you remember it all soon..
...all the details of your true selves.

About your previous lives...!
Previous lives?!
PEEP
Sailor Moon?!
Luna?!
!!
Luna?!
Are you in the command center?
Let's all go down there!
PAAA
This is just a borrowed form.
SHUUN
On Earth, I'm...
Minako Aino, a 2nd-year middle-school student, just like you all!
Nice to meet you!
Let's go!
Princess ?!

CROWN GAME CENTER
Your Highness, please accept my apologies for not being there to greet you!
Luna! What's there to apologize for? You were performing your duties just as you should!

It's been so long since I've been in this command center.

Sailor V...
I mean, Princess...
We've been searching for you all this time. But never suspected you were the princess...
But you knew about us...
Why haven't you appeared before...

Mercury...
Shall we...

...start the explanations now?

I met...
...my own partner, Artemis here, quite a long time ago.
PURR PURR
ゴロ ゴロ
That was before I knew you people even existed.
At first, Artemis and I would solve mysterious cases happening throughout Tokyo as the Champion of Justice, Sailor V.
But still, it took time for us to meet Luna and you four.
I wanted to meet up with you sooner...
...but instead decided to make a concentrated effort to study the enemy for a while longer until you all had awakened.
And while we were gathering data...
...we came to see one very large shadow behind these mysterious cases.
One strain of cases were not of human orgin. And in chasing that down...

...we discovered that the Dark Kingdom was behind it.
The one manipulating the Dark Kingdom...
...is something born of the void.
A being of pure malice.
It resembles no living thing. It is concentrated evil.

In its lust for power...
...it became aware of the sacred jewel of our Moon Kingdom, the "Legendary Silver Crystal!"

And it is now trying to take over the Earth.
Right now it is using human energy - their life force - as its power source, which is why it is targeting humanity.

Have you met it, Your Highness...?

...Long, long ago...
It was the reason that the Kingdom of the Moon...
...Silver Millennium fell, and its people never found happiness...!
It should have been buried forever... But now...!
Someone must have broken the seals...
...for something that evil to be born into this world again...!
You understand, right?
We must not allow the past to repeat itself!
This time, we must make it permanent!
We must seal it away forever!

I see...!

To make sure that past tragedies don't happen again...

...we have been reborn as guardians!

Your Highness, the "Legendary Silver Crystal" ...?

It would be too dangerous to tell you where it is safely stashed away, but...

...there are no signs that the enemy has sensed its location.

Yes, that's right! The "Legendary Silver Crystal"...

...must never fall into enemy hands...!

This is to protect the "Legendary Silver Crystal" too since the enemy will certainly target us.

We're going to fight this, everyone!

What...
...a brave, gallant princess!
It seems more like she's protecting us...!
Princess Serenity!
The Princess...
Was she like that...?
Azabu Juban Shopping District
Things are still very, very fuzzy, but...
...I get the feeling that she's much closer to us than that...
"Serenity!"

UWAAAHH !!
Endymion !!
KYAAA!!
GAMPH
わぱっ
PEEP PEEP
ぴぴ
…A dream…
CHEEP
チュン
CHEEP
チュン
I guess it's because I met the real princess that I'm having this dream.
Mmm…
He said, "Serenity"…
But when he called that name, the one who turned around was…
…me?
That guy who sometimes appears in my dreams… I called him, "Endymion."

Eh?
It's still only 6:00 AM?
I don't believe it!
ぼーっ
BWAAAH
Mm?
I'm all awake now.
YAWWWN
TMP
TMP
Ohh ?!
What's the matter? Why're you up so early...?
Always oversleeps!
It's like you aren't Usagi anymore!
Your father has already gone and run a marathon distance!
"This is just a borrowed form."
ぱっ
POP
That's right, Dad!
The you have known up until now has been just a borrowed form!
Really? Then what's your "true" form?
EH HEH HEH HEH
ぎょっ
GAK

Why, the Guardian of Love and Justice: Sailor Moon!
That's me!
Oh, ho! So that's the reason for the early rising. ♪
It's true! I may be , but I'm also Sailor Moon!
I see. I see.
Honestly, he doesn't believe me! Sniff!
...Come to think of it...
... and Sailor Moon...
I wonder which is actually the real me?
ICHI-NO-HASHI PARK
SHHHHH

...Mamoru Chiba...!
B-BMP

...Tuxedo Mask...!
... Mamo-chan.
...Ah!
B-BMP
B-BMP
B-BMP
G-Good morning.
... Yeah.
FUU
The Complete Book of Crystal
Crystal's
Treasures of
Crystal Data
Gems of the Wor

The "Legendary Silver Crystal"...

"The only clue to my past memories..."
"...are the words, "Find the 'Legendary Silver Crystal!", So I'm searching for it!"

I wonder what kind of thing it is...

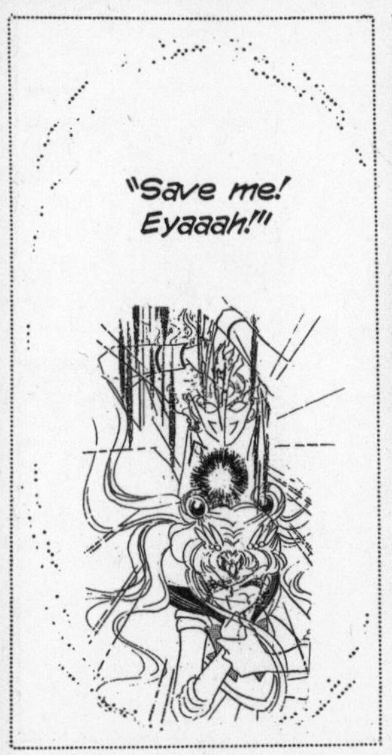

"Save me! Eyaaah!"

The "Legendary Silver Crystal" that everyone is looking for...

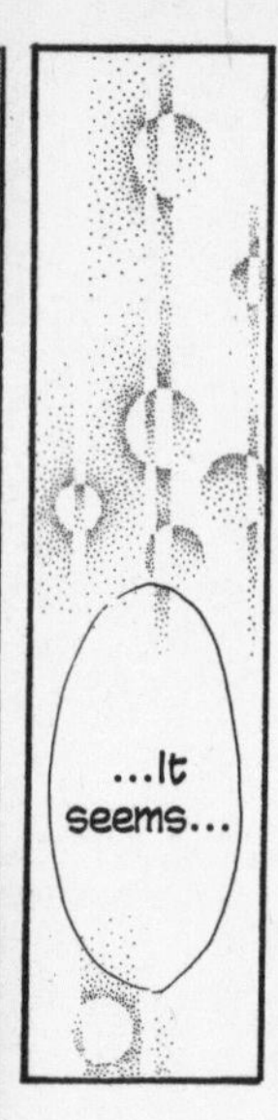
...It seems...

...that even when I don't feel I have the right to talk to you...
...it's still my destiny to meet up with you, Usako.

... Yeah. I guess so.
B-BMP
"Usako!"
B-BMP
B-BMP
Our destiny to meet...

...Um...
This watch...
It's yours, isn't it? I've been meaning to return it to you.

No. You keep it.
There's something that I really should have given back to you...
...that I still have too.

The handkerchief that you dropped during the ball a while back.

Second Year, Class One, Usagi Tsukino
I never seemed to find the chance to give it back.

Wh-What? What do you have that you need to give back?
I left something behind?

Next time.
We'll make a trade.
For sure.

...Okay!
...For sure, right?
In their own little world.
EH HEH HEH
...

SIGH
はあ
Usagi-chan is completely infatuated.
...No matter what I say now, it wouldn't get through to her.
Is he the kind of person it's all right for Usagi-chan to fall in love with? I still wonder who this guy is!
There's nothing to worry about.
Luna...
...your very first order was to find Sailor Moon and the Guardians and raise them.
But it doesn't end there. In order to ease your burden a bit...
...we did our best to avoid touching your memory lapses more than neccessary.

But originally your job was to protect Her Highness.
Now is a good time for you to know every-thing.
...Artemis?

...Ohh...
The princess of the Kingdom of the Moon ...?

Yes, Queen Metalia!

Hoping to obliterate me...
...and revive her kingdom...
...she's finally appeared!

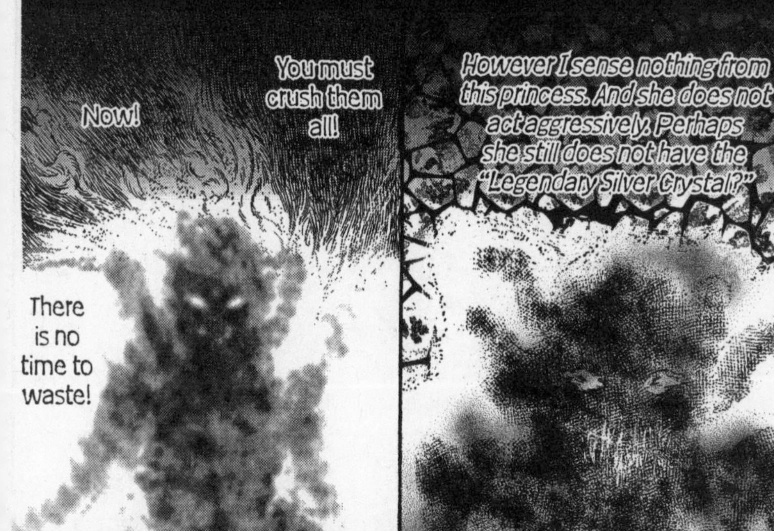

However I sense nothing from this princess. And she does not act aggressively. Perhaps she still does not have the "Legendary Silver Crystal?"
You must crush them all!
Now!
There is no time to waste!

We must find the "Legendary Silver Crystal" now and steal it for ourselves if we are to rule the Earth, Beryl!

So the Silver Millennium Princess has been reborn?

With everyone crowding around, closing in on the "Legendary Silver Crystal"...
...the battle begins anew!
...This time...
...we will be the ones to win it all! Heh heh heh...

Zoisite... I still don't believe you are re-duced to this husk...
Jadeite... Nephrite... You shrivel before my eyes...
You pitiful things...
And now, the Four Kings of Heaven...
...are down to myself alone.
With the "Legendary Silver Crystal"...
...Middle Eastern Com-mander, Kunzite...
...it would be nothing to revive them all!
I know that well, Queen Beryl.
And prior to that...
...the princess and her Sailor Guardians...
...must die.

Wow! What pretty city lights! It's so bright, it's hard to believe it's night!

It's like an open treasure chest!
The view here is wonderful! ♡
You know the type, filled with diamonds and stuff sparkling! ♡
CUDDLE いちゃ
FFT
CUDDLE いちゃ
CUDDLE いちゃ

VWOO

What an offensive, futile light.

The true beauty is within the shining darkness.
Heh!

It seems that V-chan...
No, I mean the Princess...
...lives just like a regular girl! How strange, huh? ♡
I will drag you out...
...to grovel before that darkness, Princess, Sailor Guardians!
Usagi-chan, you never have a thought in your head, do you?
The instant you transform back into Usagi-chan...
...your intelligence level takes a nosedive.
Well, doesn't Sailor Moon do the same thing?
TEE HEE
くすっ
I wish you'd stop saying things that could disillusion the princess!
It's embarrassing!
GONNG
がんっ
Rei-chan, you're awful!
You didn't have to say that!
There, there...
What's wrong with saying the truth?!
HEE HEE
くすくす
...

Look at how late it's gotten!
Heh, heh...
VZZCH
VZZCH
VZZCH
ACH
VAA
Mako-chan?!
SSST
FFFP
?!
The lights!!

Mako-chan, are you all right?!
Unh ...
A black-out?

The power lines have snapped ...!!
VZZT
VZZT
Ami, stay away from those!
Mako-chan ?!

VZZT
VZZT
Look! The people!!
SHUUU

Artemis! In one moment, all of the power supplies for Tokyo were cut off!
What was that ...?!
I can feel it! In one instant, a huge load of energy was just sucked through those wires!
The enemy ?!
Everyone, transform! I have a feeling that the enemy is near...!

Moon Prism Power...
Make up!!
The blackout goes on and on!
It couldn't be that the energy of everyone in the city was...
This is scary ...
It's the first time I've ever encountered a world so dark!

Look! There's a light coming from the very top of Tokyo Tower!!

Let's go there!
No! Princess?! Luna and Artemis are in the command center! You should escape there!
No. I'm going.
Then it's our job to *protect you!*
My heart is restless!
Tuxedo Mask?!
I hope he's all right!
...Mamoru... Mamo-chan!!
He hasn't collapsed, has he?

はっ
AH!
がばっ
GAMPH

...A dream? But who was calling me...?
My head hurts... Something's going on.

A blackout? What? That's the only place lit, and it's putting out a lot of light!

We're going up to the top!! Nobody let go!
So you've come.
Sucking up human energy! That's something even a god is forbidden to do!
WAFFT

Pretty Guardian of Love and Justice in a Sailor Suit! Sailor Moon has arrived!!
In the name of the moon, we'll punish you!
Moon Healing ...
...Esca-lation!
PAAA
KEEEN

HYUU
Sailor Moon!
I can't hold on! I'm going to fall!
CCH
FWA
Tuxedo Mask!!

You're kidding...
Again...
...he came to save me...!!
ぎゅっ
HUGG
ばっ
WHOOSH
It's dangerous here! We'll defeat the enemy!
You go as far away as you can!
SMAK

Sailor Moon...!
WHOOSH

Every time we meet, you show me a different face!
Today, you're a mighty warrior!

And what kind of girl are you really?
I wonder if there are still different versions of you?
KAK
Supreme Thunder!
Sailor Moon !
WHOOSH
Just who are you?!
Heh heh heh...
It didn't work?!
He just sucked up the electric energy?!
SHUUU

More! Give me more of your energy! And I can give it back to you hundreds of times over!
I will blow Tokyo off the map!
AH!
Run! Hurry!
He's about to attack with his built-up energy ?!
Take the princess away some-place safe!
She must be protected!
Sailor Moon!
VWAMM

Sailor Moon !!
Dam-mit!!
KAK
We have to protect Sailor Moon! Now!

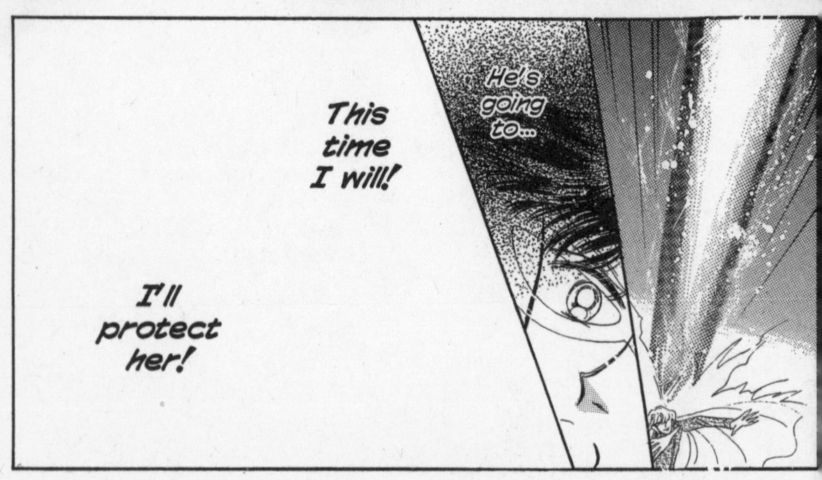
He's going to...
This time I will!
I'll protect her!

Pretty Guardian ★ Sailor Moon

Act 9
Serenity, Princess

Tuxedo Mask...?!
...somebody's calling me...

Sailor Moon?
Tuxedo Mask! Hang in there! Open your eyes!
Long hair...
She's always calling me in my dreams...
Is she... you?
You shouldn't have such a sad look on your face...
What are the tears for?
...Oh, yeah... You've done this before, haven't you?
"Endymion!"
"Endymion!"

Endymion.
That's...
...my name.
...I remember.
I was reborn into...
...the here and now......
...as Mamoru Chiba...
...so I could meet you.
Serenity ...
HAHH
No!!

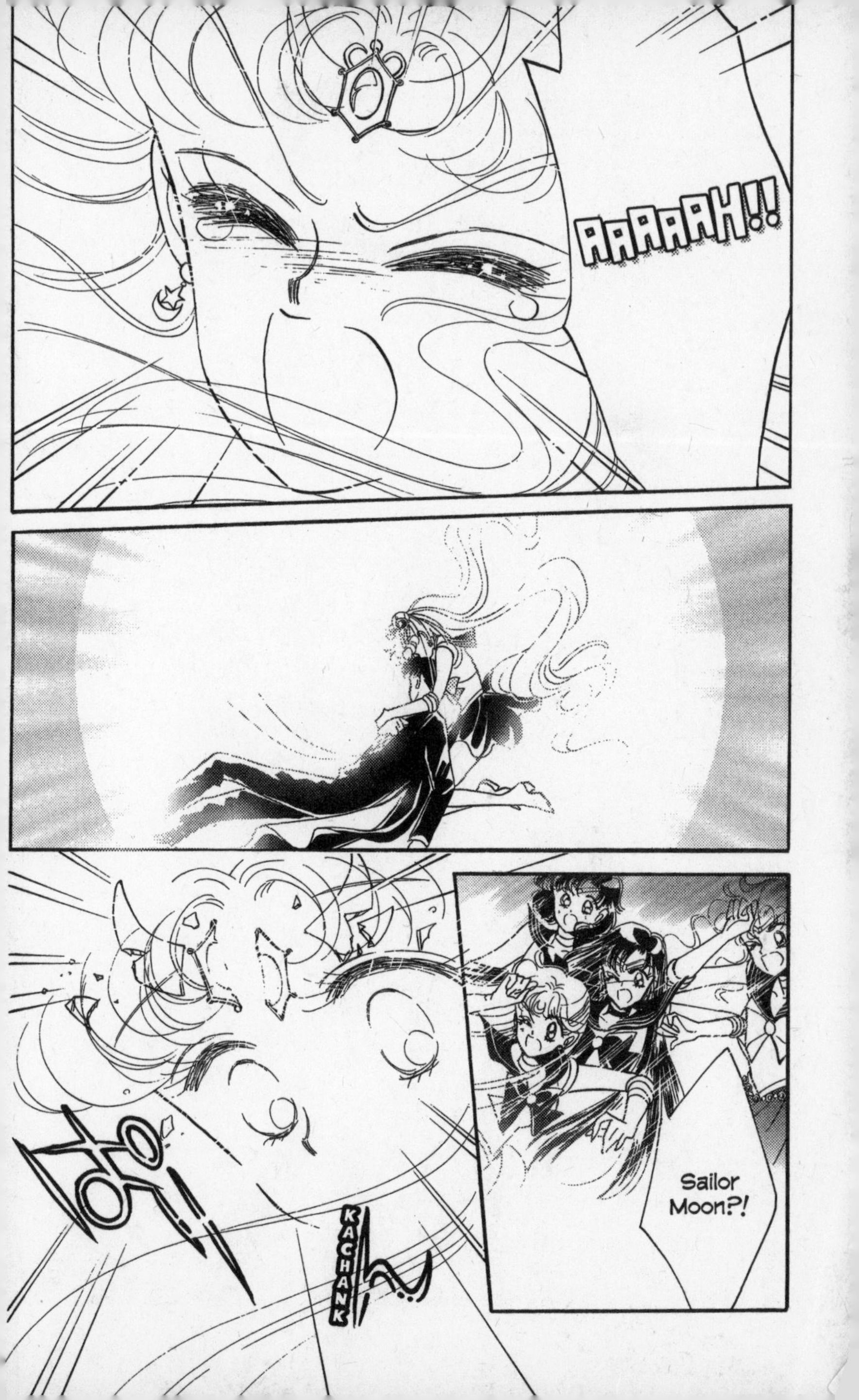
AAAAAH!!
KACHANK
Sailor Moon?!

That crescent symbol on her forehead...!
...Princess Serenity?!
PAA
POHH

FWAAA
PAAM
Tuxedo Mask's broken pocket watch...
...is starting to run backwards.
TIK
TIK
TIK
TIK
TIK
TIK
TIK

Time is going faste and farthe backwards
It's calling up the past... Calling back my memories... And carving them into me...
Sad memories keep flowing in...
It's playin then back
I remember... We were...
...Guardians assigned to protect Princess Serenity...!
We were reborn to protect the princess and to help restore the Kingdom of the Moon...
And our *real* princess is...

...I remember!
...I remember you...
I remember...
...my beloved...
...Endymion...
My memories are coming back to me one by one...
He had the same eyes as you with a deep color...
...you could just sink into.
The same deepness
the blue world in
was hidden all
our possibilities
and hopes.

Long ago, I looked at that blue planet from the moon. I loved it.
And...
...this was my secret...
...Watching Earth's prince and heir...
...that matchless strength... That marvel...
...Endymion!
I descended to the planet time and time again...
...hoping to catch a glimpse of him!
...Endymion!

...But we mustn't meet like this anymore!
...Why?
Denizens of the Earth and Moon are forbidden to fraternize.
...That is the god's law.

...I mustn't fall in love...
...but it's too late.

The Moon
WAAAA
We will take the Kingdom of the Moon and make it ours!
The "Legendary Silver Crystal" will be mine!
WAAA
Prince, will you be a traitor to Earth?
This is all for Earth's prosperity!
Stop! Lay down your arms! Stop this futile war!
GWAAH
KYAAAAA

Eyaaah!
Endymion ...!!
Talk to me... Open your eyes... Please!
I remember...
We were reborn, and I finally saw you again, but...
...is this to be our fate? Endymion!
Tuxedo Mask!!
I haven't been able to tell you anything about myself!

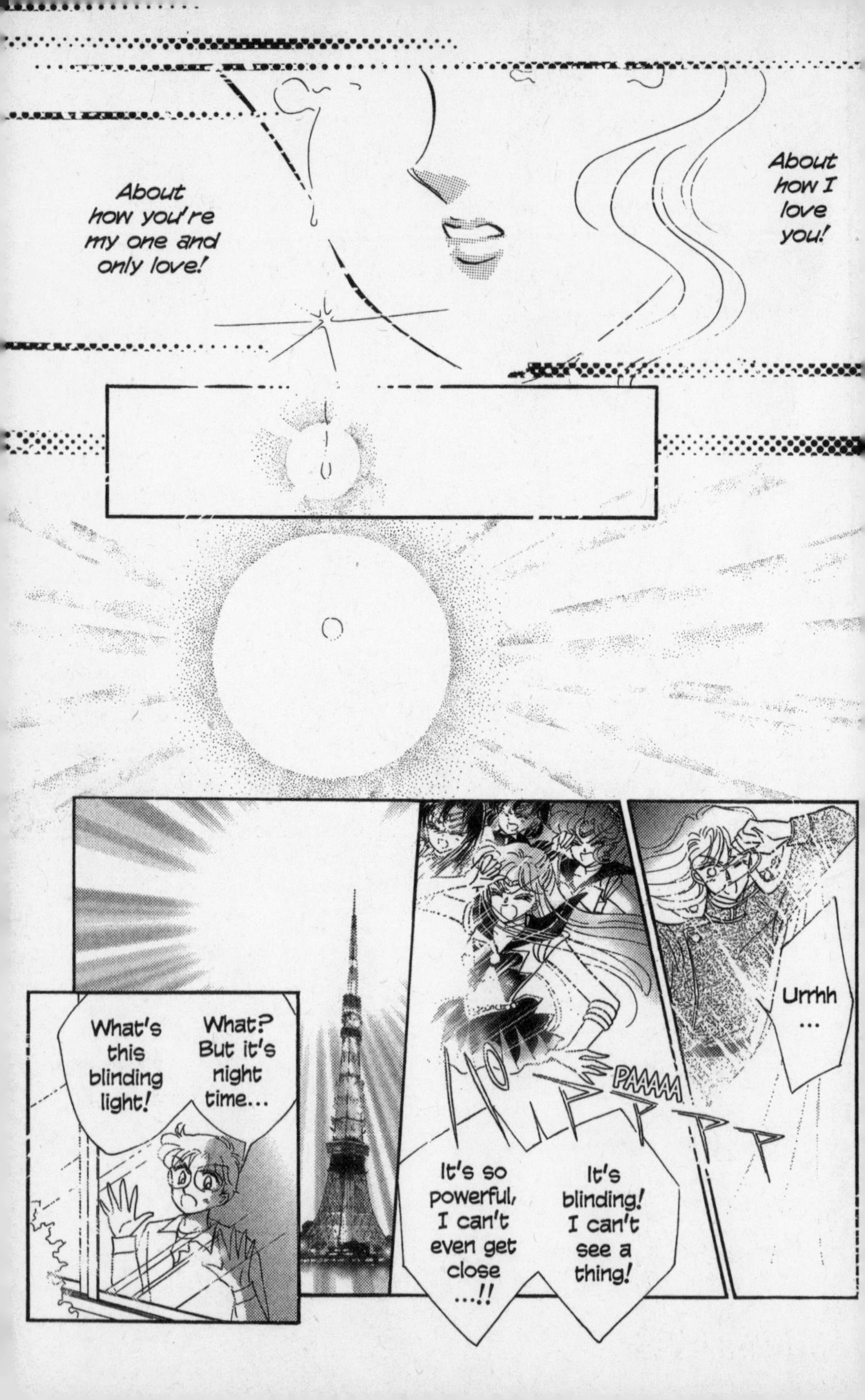
About how I love you!
About how you're my one and only love!
Urrhh ...
PAAAAA
It's blinding! I can't see a thing!
It's so powerful, I can't even get close ...!!
What? But it's night time...
What's this blinding light!

...This
light!
It's...

This is over-powering my black crystal! It'll explode!
What is this power ...?!
This extra-ordinary power ...!!
This overwhelming white light... Could it be...
...Could it be the "Legendary Silver Crystal?!"
I can see it! This light...
...is Usagi-chan's tear crystallized and shining...?!
"Legendary Silver Crystal?!"

WHEEZE
WHEEZE
KOFF
KOFF
I can't breathe...
I can't breathe...
That's...the "Legendary Silver Crystal?!"
This light... is it some new super-nova?!
My coug-hing...just stopped. I can breathe now...?!
PAAA
FWAAAH
ふわあ...
BWAAA
...No!
My barrier can't...
...hold against this... Kh...!!
What's going on here?!
The Earth's under-going a revitali-zation!
RRMMMBB
ゴゴゴゴ...

FFT
Queen Beryl!!
GWOOO
A connection has been formed between my empire and the upper world!
Ohhh...

It flows to me!
That extraordinary power, coming from above...

A sacred light is overflowing...
...my empire of darkness!

But what is this...?
Power flows in, more than I can grasp!
...I see it...!

This power! Yes, is this truly...
...the "Legendary Silver Crystal?!"
PAAA
PSSH
PASHINN
SHUUU
SHUUUU
SHUUU
AH!
Jadeite?! Nephrite?! Zoisite?! They're being revived?!
どくん B-BMP
This light... What is it?!
どくん B-BMP
...Have we just been slumbering in a very long sleep...?!
どくん B-BMP
Energy is flowing this way...
どくん B-BMP
Why are we in a place like this?
どくん B-BMP

...We should have been reborn in order to...
...find our master somewhere on Earth...
Where is our master?
Where is Endymion-sama?!
"Why do you fight?"
"Your Highness, we have had enough of being ordered around!"
"We can no longer stand the actions of the Kingdom of the Moon!"
"The way they spy on us from a distance!"
"When have you been ordered around or spied on?!"
"Whose words are you repeating?"
"That repugnant...
...creature's?!"
"Do you not see?! We are simply being made its tools!"

PASH
...What is this memory ?!
A memory from our earlier lives...?
...Yes, it is!
We were reborn...
...in order to search for our master...
...Prince Endymion-sama!
But before our memories had returned to us...

We fell once again into their hands!
And we...
...sold our-selves.
Then...
B-BMP
B-BMP
SHUUU
SHFF
Our bodies were changed.

SHUUUU
KRAKK
Zoisite, Nephrite, Jadeite...
You were changed to stone. You couldn't take it.
Look!
TWRL TWRL
くるくる
The "Legendary Silver Crystal"...

SST
すっ
AH!
TUMBL
コロン
The light went out?!
And the tremors stopped.
FFT
Kunzite, now! Steal the princess and the "Legendary Silver Crystal" for the Dark Kingdom!
BWAA
Prin-cess!!
BAA
ASH

WHUDD
FWAAA
Tuxedo Mask!!
BA
No! We can't compete with them in this state!
We have to retreat!
Princess !!
KIKK

No! Let me go! He's taking Tuxedo Mask away ...!
PAAA
Luna! Artemis! Can you hear me?!
We have to transport there! Help us out!
...He's gone?!
Nooo!! Tuxedo Mask...!
MAMO-CHAN!

CROWN GAME CENTER
CRO
TAK
カツン
...Sailor Moon...
...I mean, Princess Serenity ...
...You remember, don't you?
...About me, Sailor Venus, too?

And about how Sailor Venus was actually the leader of the Sailor Guardians assigned to protect the princess?
And about our kingdom, the Silver Millennium?
...Yes, I remember.
...Endymion...
That time, before we were reborn
Back when the Earth was its own kingdom and the Moon was a separate kingdom...
...when we were so happy...

...Eventually, the Earth and the Moon went to war.
And our period of happiness...
...was utterly destroyed.
Also...
...then, just as now...
...I was unable to save him.
I didn't suspect that Tuxedo Mask might be Endymion...
I never imagined this would happen...
Or that the enemy was never destroyed. That they still live on...
That they are still trying to dominate this planet...
There's no doubt that they're the same ones who brought our kingdom to ruin!

They're evil...
...I've heard that they are form-less, alien creatures.
And that they are hardened fragments of the void.
But we sealed them up in our past life! I know we sealed them away!
But now the seal's broken again, and she has minions following her or-ders!
That woman...
Could it be that woman who broke the seal...?!
And she's the one running the Dark Kingdom?!
We have to locate the Dark Kingdom!
That thing that was sucked into the body of Tuxedo Mask was a portion of the "Legendary Silver Crystal," right?
If we don't act fast, this could be a dis-aster!
B-BMP
...I don't...

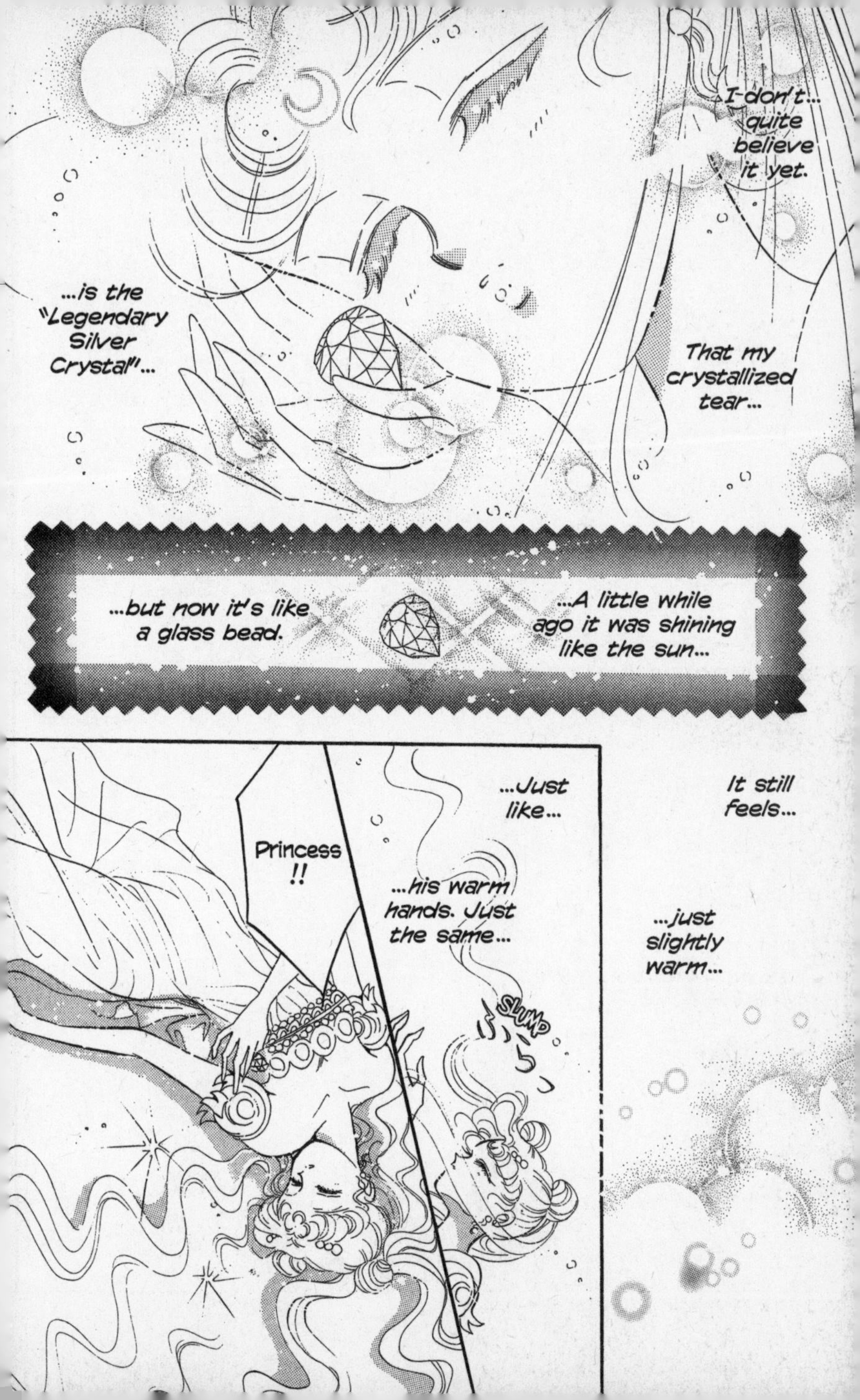

I-don't... quite believe it yet.
That my crystallized tear...
...is the "Legendary Silver Crystal"...
...A little while ago it was shining like the sun...
...but now it's like a glass bead.
It still feels...
...just slightly warm...
...Just like...
...his warm hands. Just the same...
SLUMP
Princess !!

Hasn't he awakened yet?!
B-BMP
...ドクン
B-BMP
...ドクン

His heart is beating at normal strength.
He is weakened, however...
...there is a special power flowing within his body.

But no matter where we look in his body, we cannot find anything similar to the "Legendary Silver Crystal!" What's the meaning of this?!

I know what I saw! The "Legendary Silver Crystal" let out a light which was sucked into his body! Is it supposed to have dispersed within his body?! Why doesn't it register...?!

GWUP
ムクッ

A body with no trace of the "Legendary Silver Crystal"...
...is of no use to me!

DOLUUNN
Eyaaah!
WHOOSH
ざっ
HAHH
はあ
HAHH
はあ
SHIVER
がく
SHIVER
がく
...A dream...!
HAHH
はあ
I wonder how many times...
...I've woken up...
...my eyes wet with tears?
...Tuxedo Mask...!

SIGH はあ。
My eyes are as red as a bunny's.
Or rath- er...
...so puffy they could be Chinese Manju dumpling buns!
Too much crying!
What a face!
FLIFF さらっ
CROWN GAME CENTER
CRO
...I wonder how much time has passed.
I am...
...Luna, protector of Princess Serenity.
I made a vow never to leave the princess's side no matter what.
...But here I am. And this is the first time I've ever been away from Usagi-chan this long.
I re- member now.
...I was...
...left sleeping for a very long time along with Artemis...
...following the destruction of the Moon Kingdom.

Then eventually we awakened...
...and descended down to Earth.
My first order was to awaken Sailor Moon...
...raise her and watch over her.
The reason my memory was sealed...
...and that Sailor Venus was presented as a body-double princess...
...as well as training Usagi-chan for her part as Sailor Moon...
...was all to protect the princess...
...and protect that which was hidden within her...
...the "Legendary Silver Crystal!"
...We were hoping we could deceive the enemy a little longer than we did.

But...
...her awakening happened in a way we didn't anticipate.
If only I had gotten my memories back sooner...
...and realized that Tuxedo Mask was actually Endymion...
...it would have ended without such pain for Usagi-chan.
...I should have trusted Usagi-chan more.
...But my actions led to her present sorrow.
I'm a failure as Usagi-chan's partner.
If you're her partner...
...you should be with her.
Artemis!
Sorry. I'm not being very much like me, am I?
Have you been here all this time?
I've been investigating the location of the Dark Kingdom, but I can't seem to find any leads.
How is Usagi-chan?

Oh, you're here!
We're so sorry she's a daily worry for you!
Hello! Is Usagi-chan available?
It's been a week already, and her school work...
That's true...We should at least force her to go to school.
Nothing's changed. She won't step foot outside of her room.
She hardly eats even a bite.
She must have suffered some great shock. I wonder what it was...
たっ TMP
Ah!
It's the crescent bald-spot kitty-chan! I haven't seen it for a while.
It must be worried about Usagi too.
Usagi's Room
Usagi-chan, are you all right?

It's me! Luna! Open up!
TONK TONK
Usagi-chan?
コンコン
カチャ KACHAK
KREE
...Luna...
SHFFF
...Everybody...
Usagi-chan?!
Your hair...?!

It was extremely long when I was a princess, huh?
After probably one more twist and her bun should be finished.
It's probably because your memory returned so quickly that your body underwent a change.
SNIPP
It's been growing like crazy since that night.
...A change...?
Am I becoming the princess? It's like I've stopped being me...
Where is the "Legendary Silver Crystal?" You still have it?
Yeah, but...
...it hasn't shown any signs of change.
Is this really the "Legendary Silver Crystal?"

Back then, it was shining like the sun.
Say, at the time...
...didn't it lose whatever was inside it and get sucked up into the body of Tuxedo Mask?
Isn't there a secret somehow connected to that?
ZHAAN
...Tuxedo Mask?!
Where ...
...is he now?!
We have to defeat the Dark Kingdom!
We need to rescue him!
Usagi-chan?!
If we don't, his body will continue to wither away... Noooo!
Endymion!
Usagi-chan?!

Princess!! Snap out of it!!
We're right here with you!
Our lives are dedicated to serving you!
We'll all help you get him out of there!
...So please...! Stop your crying...!
Return to the bright, happy girl you were! Okay?
I was...
I was the very last inheritor...
...of the throne of Silver Millennium...
Princess Serenity.
...I have to snap out of this!

I have to save him!
...He's still alive! I just know it!
...I need to know where the Dark Kingdom is.
...I also need to know the secret behind the "Legendary Silver Crystal."
...But...
...I don't know anything! I have no clue!
What'll I do ...?!
Let's go to the moon.
Eh?!
Let's go to where our kingdom used to be.

To discover the truth behind all the secrets...
To the moon!!

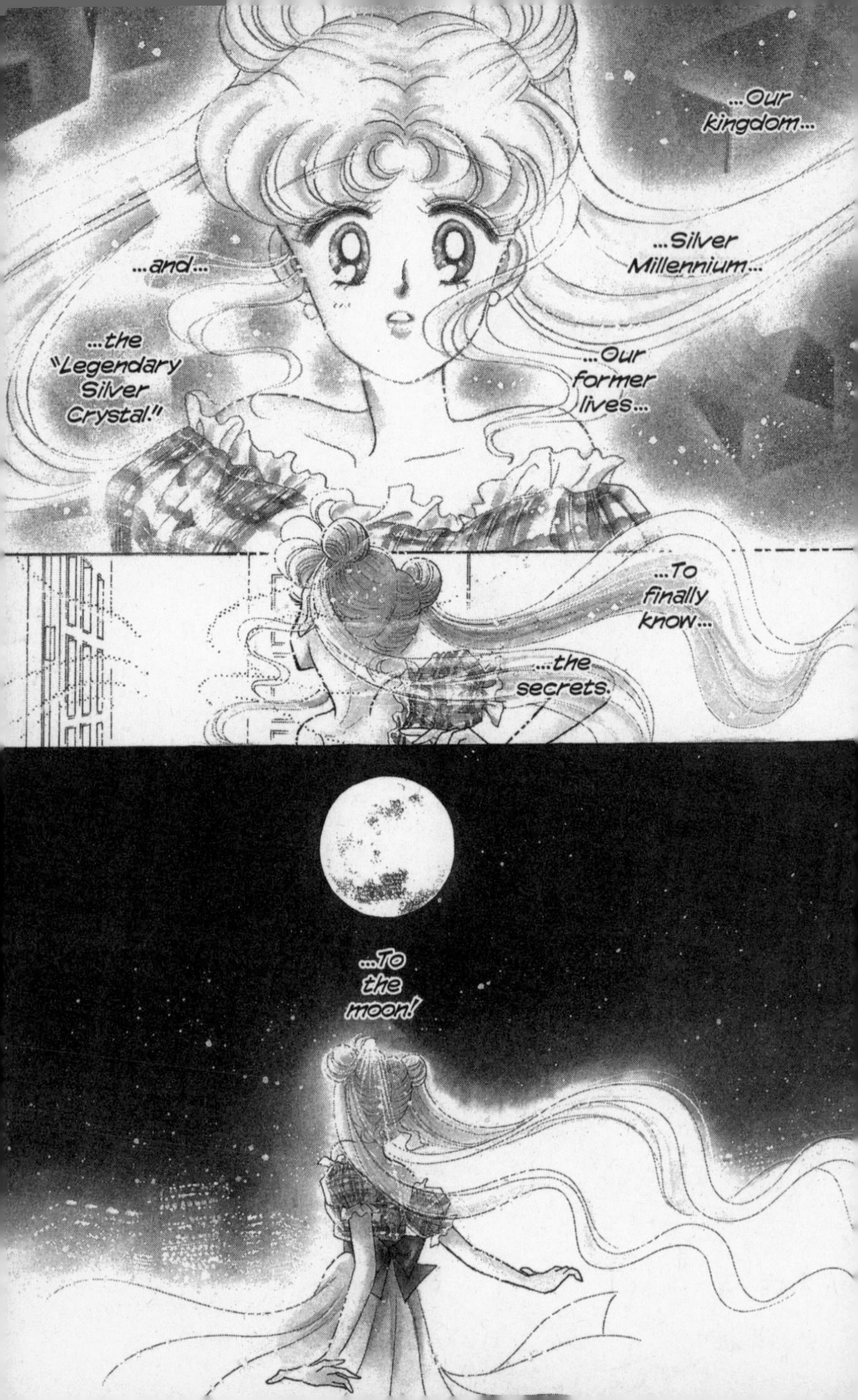
...Our kingdom...
...Silver Millennium...
...Our former lives...
...and...
...the "Legendary Silver Crystal."
...To finally know...
...the secrets.
...To the moon!

Pretty Guardian
Sailor Moon
Act 10
Moon

Now that we've decided to do it, we should start the planning.
Let's set it...
...on the night of the next full moon. That would be best.

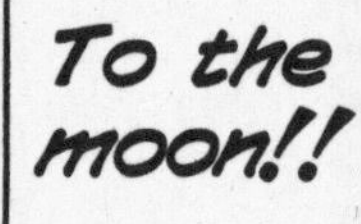
To the moon!!

CROWN GAME CENTER

The moon
"The moon..."
"It's mass is one-eightieth of the Earth's; gravity on the surface is one-sixth that of Earth's; and it's diameter is one-fourth of the Earth's."
"It is Earth's satellite, and it takes approximately twenty-eight days to make one complete orbit."
Escape Velocity
Earth: 11.2 kms
Moon: 2.4 kms
Luna's suggestion of going to the moon was easily said, but I wonder how she intends for us to go about getting there?
Usagiii! Come over here!
ヒューン
OPYUUN
Hurry up!
ガガガガ
GAM GAM GAM GAM
It's nice to see Usagi-chan looking better.
きゃははっ
GYA HA HA
I don't think she can stay depressed for long.
After all, we're going to the moon.

The moon is getting fuller and fuller.
And together with that, my feelings grow stronger and stronger.
I want to hurry to the moon and learn about my former life.
Usagi! Dinner!
Okay!
Usagi!
...Learn everything!
I have to come to his rescue as soon as possible...
You wanted this made into a pendant, right? Here it is.
Yaay!

えっ!? EH!?
... Yeah...
Nooo!
がーん GONNG
You're treating it like it's something precious.
Did you get it from someone you're in love with?
にやにや HEHN HEHN
Something like that, anyway...
Sigh... My eyes are tired from staring at a monitor all the time.
Today is my day to take time off!
トコ TUMP
トコ TUMP
Tsukino
...Say, Mother?
What is it, Father?
It's so warm and comfy in the lap of 's mom!
ゴロゴロ PURR PURR

Doesn't sometimes look like a different person?
Like before we know it, she's become an adult and will vanish from the house soon...
That won't happen!
will always be our little spoiled daughter!
PIKON PIKON
JAJING
...
Mako-chan, I'll have Oolong tea!
Okay!
I'll have plum juice!
Tonight you and I are staying over at Mako-chan's place, Rei!
The moon's stage is 13.7.
PEEP
Only one more day until the full moon.

Is everyone in top shape?
Then let's go to the park.
The park?
ドキン
B-BMP
...This place...
...is where Mamo-chan and I made the promise to trade this watch for whatever he has...
...The times when I'd meet him by coincidence on the street...

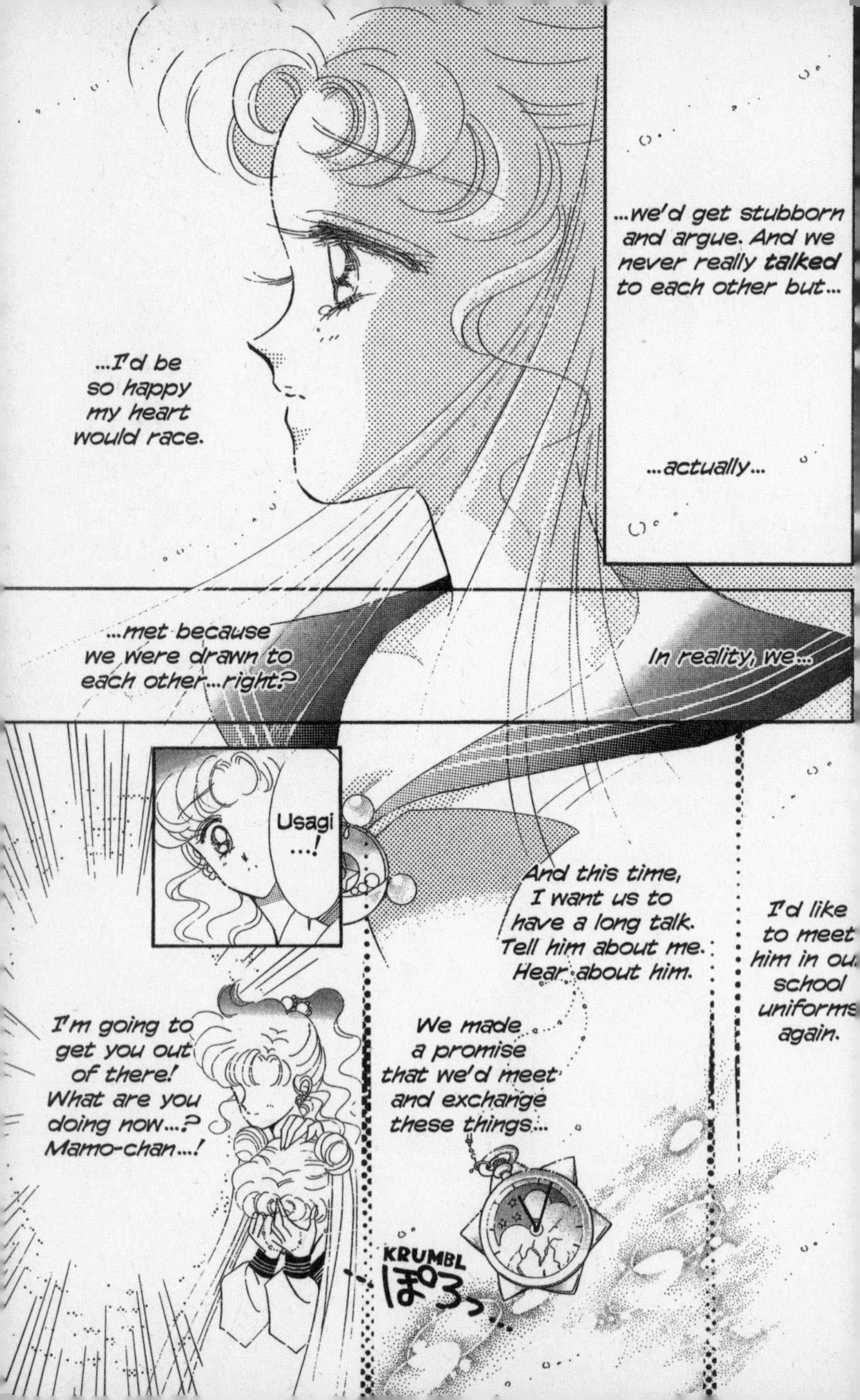
...we'd get stubborn and argue. And we never really **talked** to each other but...
...actually...
...I'd be so happy my heart would race.
In reality, we...
...met because we were drawn to each other...right?
I'd like to meet him in ou school uniforms again.
And this time, I want us to have a long talk. Tell him about me. Hear about him.
Usagi ...!
We made a promise that we'd meet and exchange these things...
KRUMBL
ぽろっ
I'm going to get you out of there! What are you doing now...? Mamo-chan...!

PBBBT
Moon phase: 15.
It's directly above this park too. And crystal-clear skies without a cloud in sight. Perfect for going to the moon.
Partial moons indicate malice and discord. New moons indicate death and destruction.
If you want a vision of the future, the full moon is best.
FLAFF
FLAFF
I can feel extra strength in this white light.
Let's transform. That's the power we'll use to translocate ourselves.
POHH
Now, enter into the center of the circle and transform.
Once you've transformed, everyone, link hands.
We'll be making a shield.
POHH

Moon Prism Power!!
Mercury Power!
Mars Power!
Jupiter Power!
Venus Power!
Make up!!

...Amaz-
ing...
That's
Earth...
...Mako-
chan,
look!

You can see flashes of light-ning!
It's like a dream. Is this the planet we were on just moments ago...?
Look!
The moon! ...It really is covered in craters.
Just like Mercury.
Where are we touching down, Luna?
"Mare Serenitatis."
...To the "Sea of Serenity."
FWAA

...This is the moon...!
...It's so dark!
...And not a sound. It feels so weird!

HUGG ぎゅっ

Say, Usagi...
Here's a true...

Moon Bunny!
SLUMP へなっ
SLIPP ずりっ

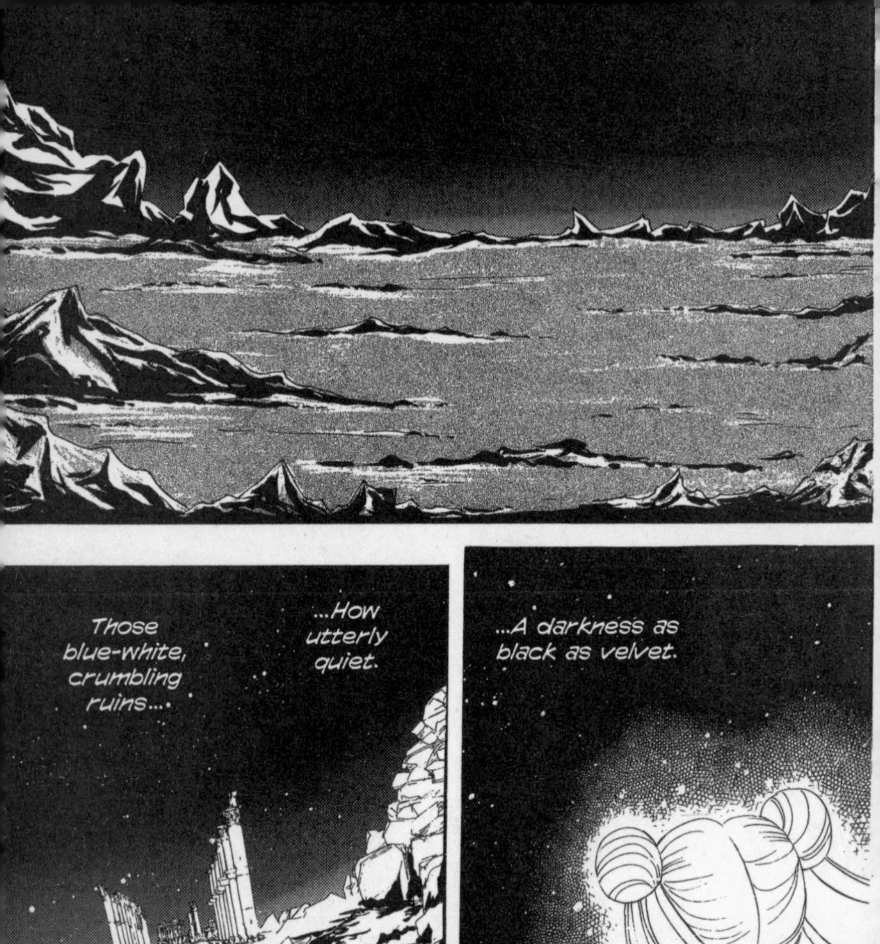
...A darkness as black as velvet.
...How utterly quiet.
Those blue-white, crumbling ruins...

...This is the moon...

Silver Millennium.
This is where our kingdom was.
Look at all the broken columns ...
This area was where the temple was?
Yes.
This was called the Moon Castle.

And these here ...
...are the remains of the Chamber of Prayer, into which only the queen could enter.
...And here was the very heart of the Moon Castle...
...the Crystal Tower.

...What's that...?
Mars, Mercury, Jupiter, Venus, each of you, draw the sword.
A sword in the stone? The whole thing's fossilized! Not possible!
Right!
GRRN
GRRN
GRRN
Put in all your strength! You should be able to do it!

I got it out?!
PAA
TUGG
AA
POHH
...ポワッ
Luna, thank you for bringing everybody here.
Mercury, Mars, Jupiter and Venus, this belongs to you.
That is the sacred sword of legends that protects the princess.
The former queen of Silver Millennium, Queen Serenity.
...the incarnation of the Moon goddess Selene.
To the people of Earth, I am called...

Queen Serenity...?!
Cute little Serenity.
That's you, right?
I can see you well.
From my past life...
...this was my mother...?
This isn't just a recording?
This image is created through combining computers with my past memories.
Using the Eternity Main System in the Moon Castle...
...my will lives on even though my body has long since turned to dust.
I put Luna and Artemis into cold sleep...
...then awakened them to watch over you all. I've been waiting a very long time for this moment.

It's all been turned to ruins now, but...
...do you remember?
When the Moon Castle was beautiful?
Yes, it was under domes, but wind blew through the greenery...
Still, Serenity, you preferred...
...the more natural wind and trees...
...and often went down to Earth.
There you found love.
"Princess!"
Kyaa!
"Did you secretly go down to Earth again?!"
"You're set to inherit Silver Millennium! There are a ton of things you have to study before then!"

...It's true..
I wanted t
see him...
...so I set distractions so I could go down to Earth often.
We are a long-lived race born on the moon.
We protect the sacred stone handed down in the Moon's royal family, the "Legendary Silver Crystal."
Our mission is to remove the disturbing factors from the Earth...
...and instead to encourage, provide rescue and guide the Earth to evolve in the best manner possible.
Even now the memory is clear.
Father Sun was at the time wracked with extraordinary activity.
The sun let out a strange glow...
...that had never been seen before.

That abnormal Sun...
...brought disaster to the solar system.
Alien creatures invaded the Earth and tried to make that beautiful planet their own.
That alien life was humanity's enemy... No, the enemy of all that exists. Evil in its purest form.
And...
...they were not content with simply the Earth...

...they sought domination of the wonderous stone and its limitless power, the sacred relic of the Moon, the "Legendary Silver Crystal."
...Making use of those dark places deep in the bottom of the human heart, they manipu-lated the people...
...and attacked the moon.
At the time, the young-yet-strong prince, Endymion...
...he alone remained immune to the enemy's lies, and fought long and hard to protect his people.

But he was too late.
Protecting you...
...he fell...
...and in your despair, you decided to take your own life.
Do you remember that?
After that, I was finally able to seal it away...
...but in the process, this Moon Castle was turned to stone in its entirety and crumbled into ruin.
At the same time, the Earth's kingdom fell as well, and once again, the Earth was left to evolve.
...That was a tale of the ancient past.
But the evil creatures have been revived.

Back then, the shock of losing you...
...despair...
...confusion...
...in my weakness, I could not entirely use the power of the "Legendary Silver Crystal."
There's no telling where those creatures are hiding.
But they are at work in the deep recesses of the Earth.
And because I could not use the crystal's full power...
...the seal on that evil creature was imperfect.
So this time...
...we must cause it to vanish completely!
We must use the true power of the "Legendary Silver Crystal!"
Princess! Only you have the ability to wipe the evil from existence!

The true power of the "Legendary Silver Crystal?"
Your Majesty! The "Legendary Silver Crystal" is acting strangely!
What was inside seemed to be sucked into Prince Endymion...
...then it lost its glow and hasn't returned since!
What was inside was sucked in...? Does that mean...
...you wanted...
...to save him, Princess Serenity...
...and in that moment, you exorcized your will. Is that it?
...You were so worried, and the anxiousness showed in your eyes, didn't it, Serenity?
It'll be fine.
He's alive, I'm sure of it. Relax.

...Yes...
Princess Serenity, remember this well.
The "Legendary Silver Crystal" depends on your heart.
I'm sure...
...he's still alive.
A strong determination, iron will and deep feelings of love...
Without all of these, you cannot hope to eliminate the evil.
You are a princess and the guardian of love and justice, Sailor Moon. Have confidence and pride in these facts.

Also never forget that you are a normal girl too.
The true reason why you were reborn is found there as well...
... mber that...
VZZT
PEEEP
ZHHG
Your Majesty ?!
Mercury, Mars, Jupiter and Venus...
...please combine your strength to protect the princess...
...and bring back this king-dom...
WAVERR
...and this Moon Castle...
I'm almost out of power... I can only speak for...
...another moment or two...
Serenity ...
...I wish you... all the happiness...
WAVERR
Your Majesty?!

Wait! If you need power, this can...
Your Majesty ?!
カラン
CLANK
...Just when I need it...
...the "Legendary Silver Crystal" lets me down.
The power of the "Legendary Silver Crystal"...
...depends on my heart...?
It looks like soon, morning will be coming to the Earth... We have to go back.
...The Earth...
...looks like a glass ball decoration that hangs on a Christmas tree...

…フッ
FFT
SHAA
さあっ
...There's a sounc
spreading out tha
can never be hear
on the moon.
...The wide-open sea.
The wind bringing the fragrance of nature.
We weren't "observing" the Earth.
We constantly dreamed of this planet, loved it...
...and watched over it.

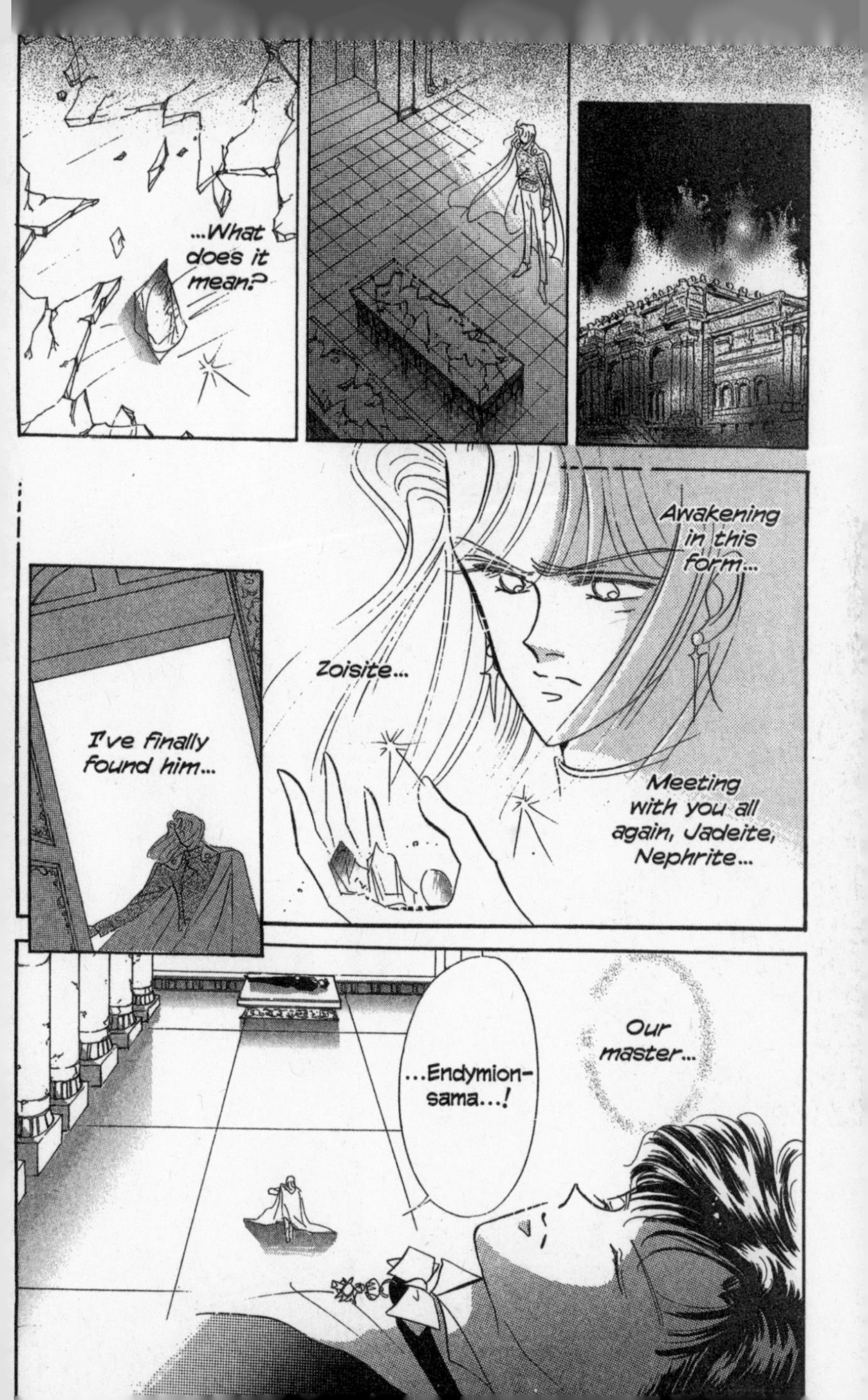
...What does it mean?
Awakening in this form...
Meeting with you all again, Jadeite, Nephrite...
Zoisite...
I've finally found him...
Our master...
...Endymion-sama...!

!
Queen Beryl?!
חודו תמורתו אחד
GM GM GM GM GM
Was there actually a door this deep within the Earth?
...What?! What is that heavy, foul... putrid smell...? I can't breathe!
AH!

GWOOOO
What is...
...that mark on her fore-head...?
!
SHF

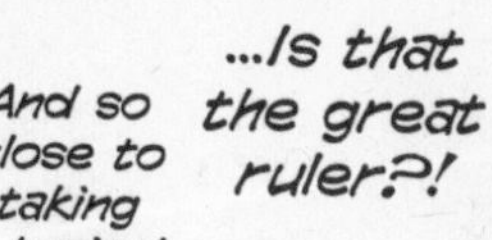
...Is that the great ruler?!
And so close to taking physical form?!

Queen Metalia...
I cannot help but be con-vinced...
...that the power of the "Legendary Silver Crystal" sucked into Tuxedo Mask has now vanished.
No trace of it registers.

Then render him into a corpse!
The "Legendary Silver Crystal" is in the hands of the Princess.

There are still benefits to using the body of Tuxedo Mask.

I imagine that Kunzite will not hold out for long.
Please leave their disposal to me.

Beryl, I need much, much more energy!
Now that the princess is fully awakened, we haven't a moment to spare if we wish to make this world ours!

You must eliminate all who would interfere...
And steal the "Legendary Silver Crystal!"

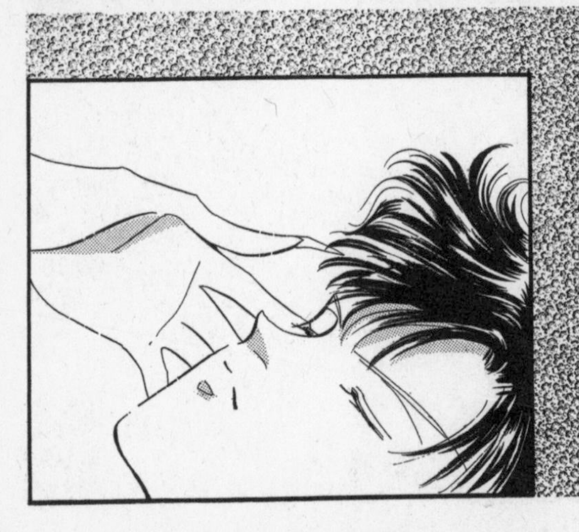

Queen Beryl...

I thought you said...
...that if you got your hands on the "Legendary Silver Crystal" that we Four Kings of Heaven would be revived.

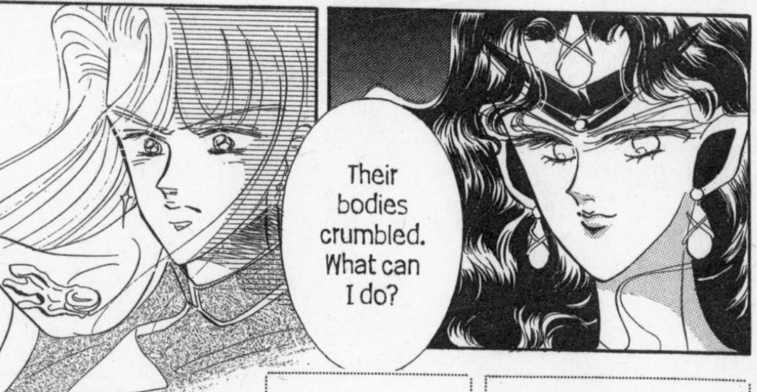
Their bodies crumbled. What can I do?

"Kyaaaa! Endymion!!"

Are you saying that the moment we chose the path that took us into the clutches of evil...
it became
oo late for
regrets?
The prince! What do you intend to do with the body of Endymion...?

VWAK
SST
Or that you have given your body to me!
You may be reborn again and again, but you Four Kings of Heaven will always be my minions!
Never forget the words of your vow to our great ruler!
Now, go! Kunzite!
This time, no failure will be tolerated!
Attack the humans and empty them of their energy!
That will certainly draw the Princess out!
Then you must steal the "Legendary Silver Crystal!"

SHUSH
SHUSH
SHUSH
WOOOSH
KYAAA!
What?! The sea?! A tsunami?!
CHIK
PA
PCHIK
KRAKL KRAKL
KRAKK KRAKK
There are people frozen in there!
RRRT
RRRT
This is an emergency announcement...
Heh heh heh... I will turn all of Tokyo into a desert of ice!
A desert of ice and gathered energy! Our great ruler will be so pleased!
Now Princess and your lackeys, show yourselves!

CROWN GAME CENTER
CRO W
PEEP ピッ
PEEP ピッ
The Earth's crust has become much more active recently.
PEEP ピッ
PEEP ピッ
There's a very slight, but odd, heat reading coming from the region of the North Pole.
PEEP ピッ
PEEP ピッ
And it's deep under-ground.
For the past several months, its data points have been all over the place.
It's possible this has something to do with the Dark Kingdom …
VWEET
VWEET
Luna! Everybody, it's the enemy! Look!
The streets are freezing over!
What did you say?!
Everybody, scramble!
Hurry up and trans-form!

Moon Prism Power...
Make up!
You're late, Sailor Moon...
...or rather, Princess!
He's...
You're trying to turn Tokyo into the North Pole?!
Exactly! So that we can revive our great ruler!
That's not going to happen!
Moon Healing...
AA
VWAA

Escalation!
SHUUN
GLEEM
!!
There! The "Legendary Silver Crystal!!"
!!
VWAA

Sailor Moon!!
If I keep moving upwards...!
FFT
FFT
Where have you taken Tuxedo Mask?!
Give him back! You'd better hope he's unharmed!
I'll give him back if you'll just hand over the "Legendary Silver Crystal" like a good girl.
HEH HEH
VWMM

Heh heh!
As a corpse!
KAA
Sailor Moon!!
Heh heh... Can your attacks have any effect in the vacuum of space?
Now, I think the first one to eliminate is this princess here!
Too bad for you, but this is our second time in space!
We're going to combine our strengths, okay? Venus Power!
Mercury Power!
Mars Power!
Jupiter Power!

Sailor Moon! Use your stick to erect a barrier for yourself!
NOO!!
I`still haven't heard about Tuxedo Mask!
PAA
Sailor Planet Attack!
AA
KRMBL
Sailor Moon!
Are you all right?

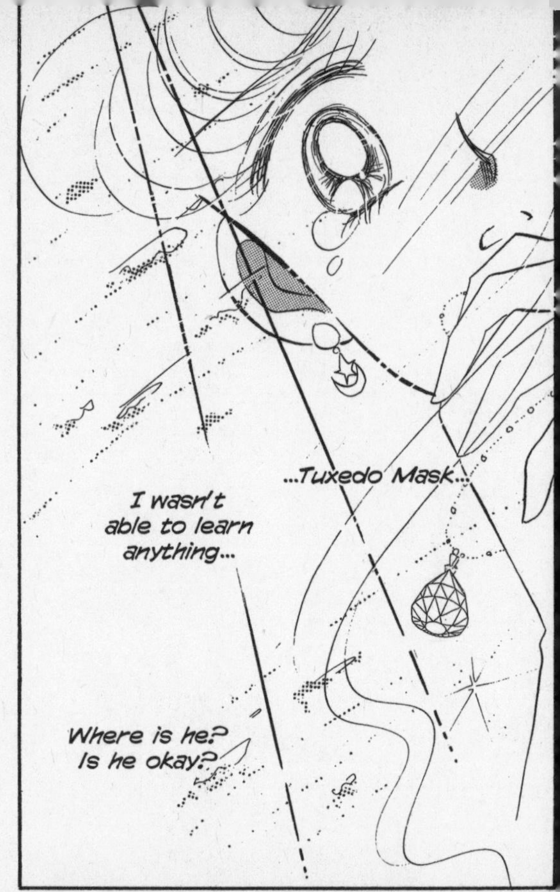
...Tuxedo Mask...
I wasn't able to learn anything...
Where is he? Is he okay?

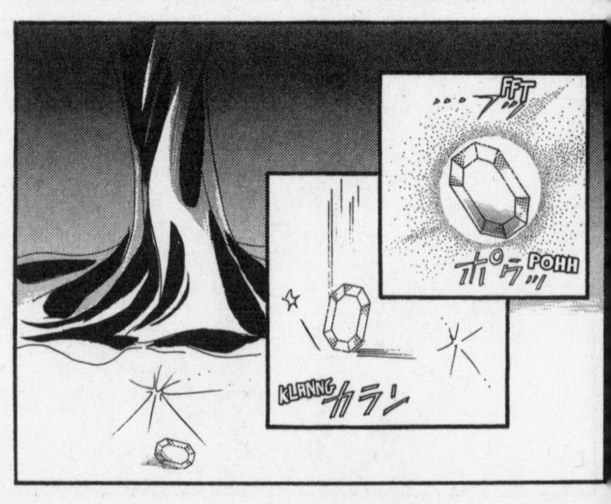
FFT
POHH
KLANNG

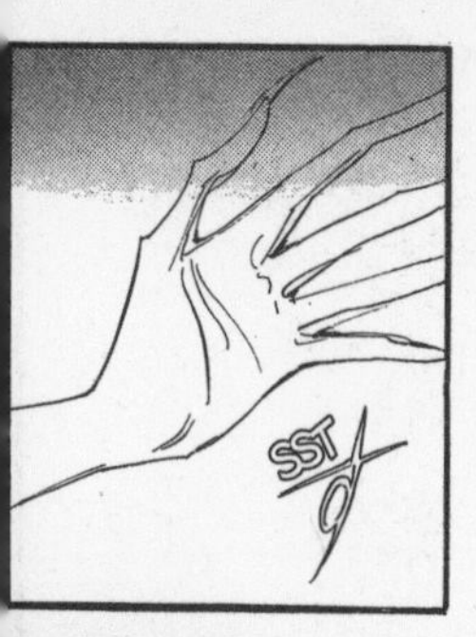

Now the bodies of all my sweet Four Kings of Heaven have crumbled and turned to stone.

Kunzite, you pathetic fool!

Your power...
...I call on my great ruler, Queen Metalia...
...grant it to me!

The power to awaken!

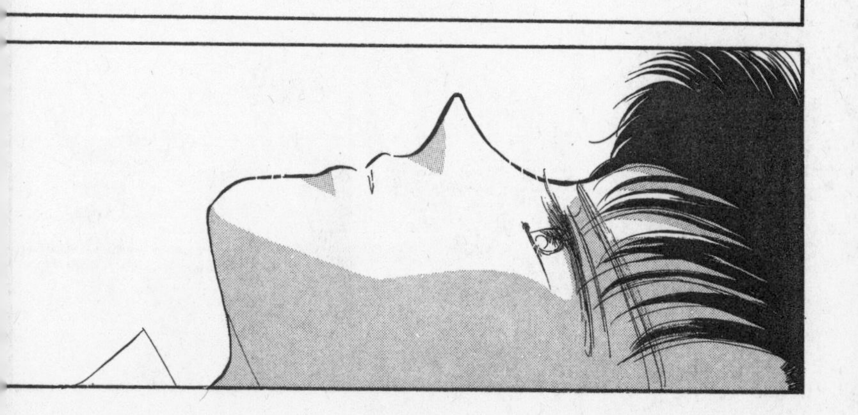

FUU
...

Prince Endymion...

You are now the puppet of Queen Beryl!

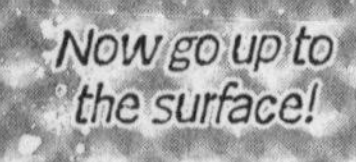
Now go up to the surface!

Your orders are to murder the princess of the Kingdom of the Moon, Silver Millennium...
...and to steal the "Legendary Silver Crystal!"

VRRRMM
BEEP BEEP BEEP
ざわ CHATTER
ざわ CHATTER
CROWN GAME CENTER
CROWN
KAK

Pretty Guardian ★ Sailor Moon

Act 11
Reunion, Endymion

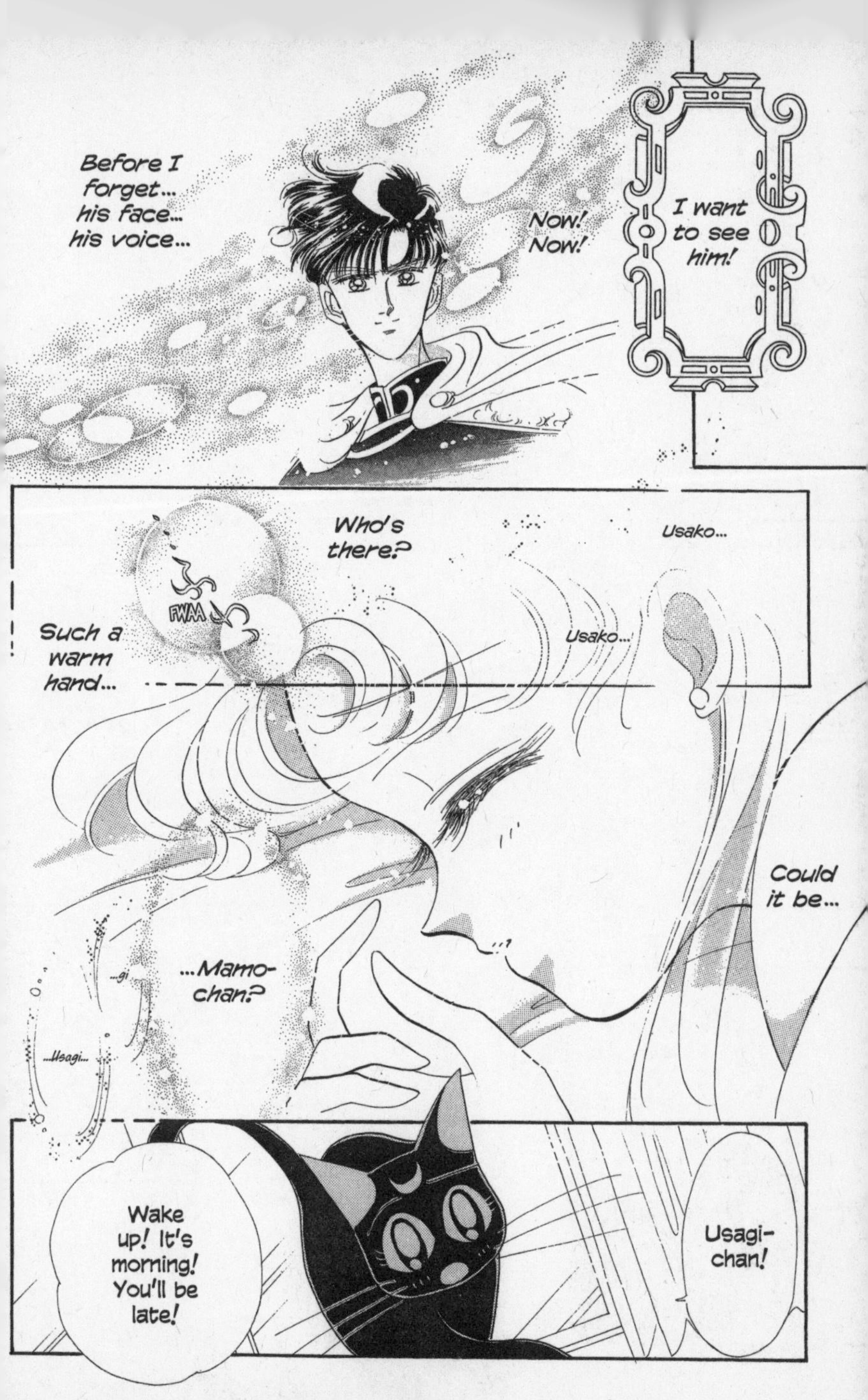
I want to see him!
Now! Now!
Before I forget... his face... his voice...
Usako...
Who's there?
Usako...
FWAA
Such a warm hand...
Could it be...
...Mamo-chan?
...gi
...Usagi...
Usagi-chan!
Wake up! It's morning! You'll be late!

…ぱちっ
BLINK
…Luna?
がーんっ
GONNG
Oh, it's just you, Luna?
What do you mean, "just?!" That's awful!
It was just getting to the good part!
Tuxedo Mask's…
Mamo-chan's broken pocket watch…
It's stopped when we re-turned from the Moon…
Right now, is he… all right?
しゅん
SLUMP
Fine! Fine! It's just me, after all!
Luna! ♡
I'm sorry! I really love you! ♡
I'll wake up.
ぎゅ
HUGG
Usagi-chan, here. You're forgetting this.

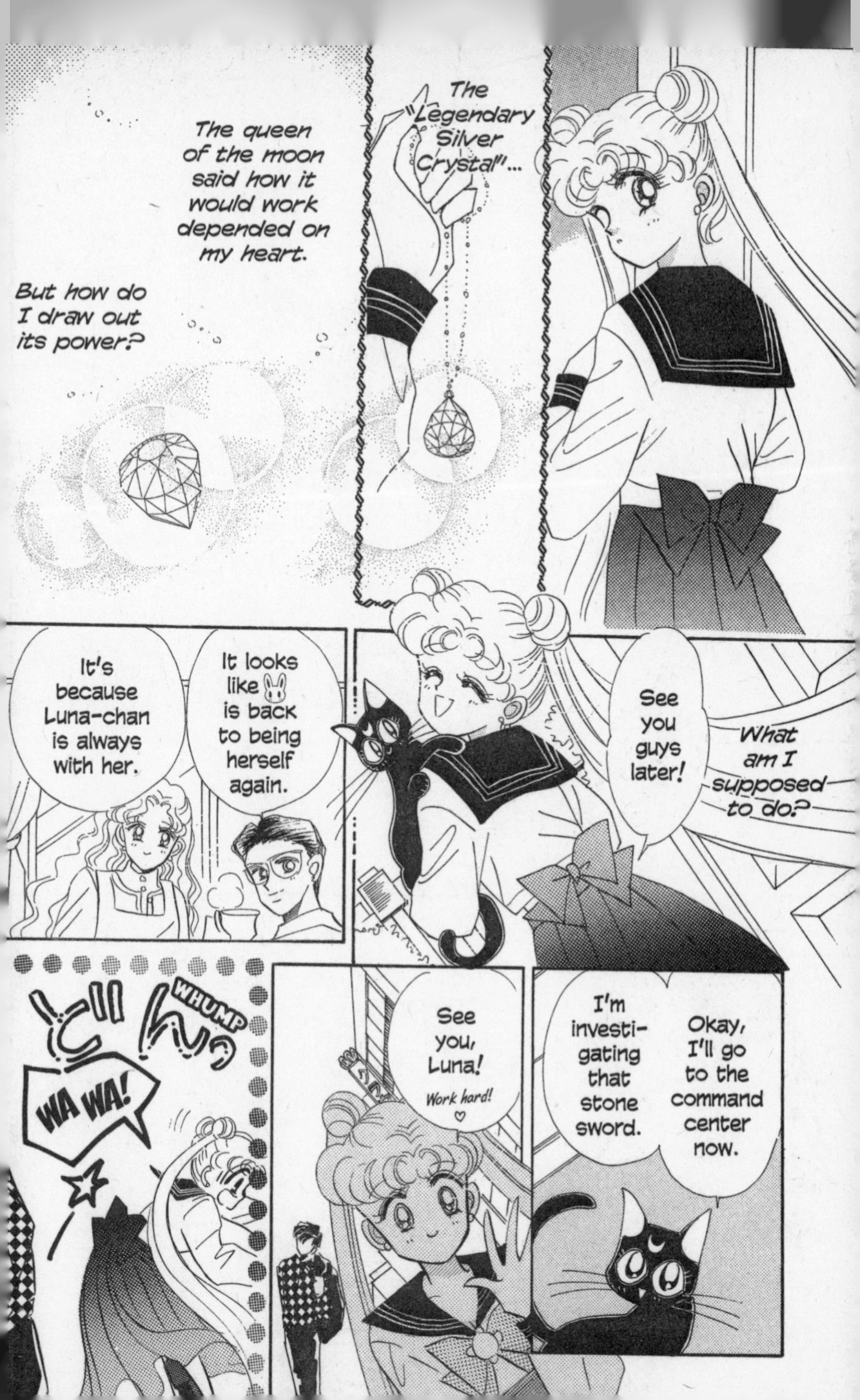

The "Legendary Silver Crystal"...
The queen of the moon said how it would work depended on my heart.
But how do I draw out its power?
What am I supposed to do?
See you guys later!
It looks like is back to being herself again.
It's because Luna-chan is always with her.
Okay, I'll go to the command center now.
I'm investi-gating that stone sword.
See you, Luna! Work hard! ♡
WHUMP
WA WA!

KACHANK
That hurrrt!
B-BMP
AH!
...From behind, he looks...
...just like him!
...But he couldn't be...
There's no way it could be him!
Oh, geez! This is because I had a dream about him this morning!
B-BMP
KIK
Like him...
B-BMP
B-BMP

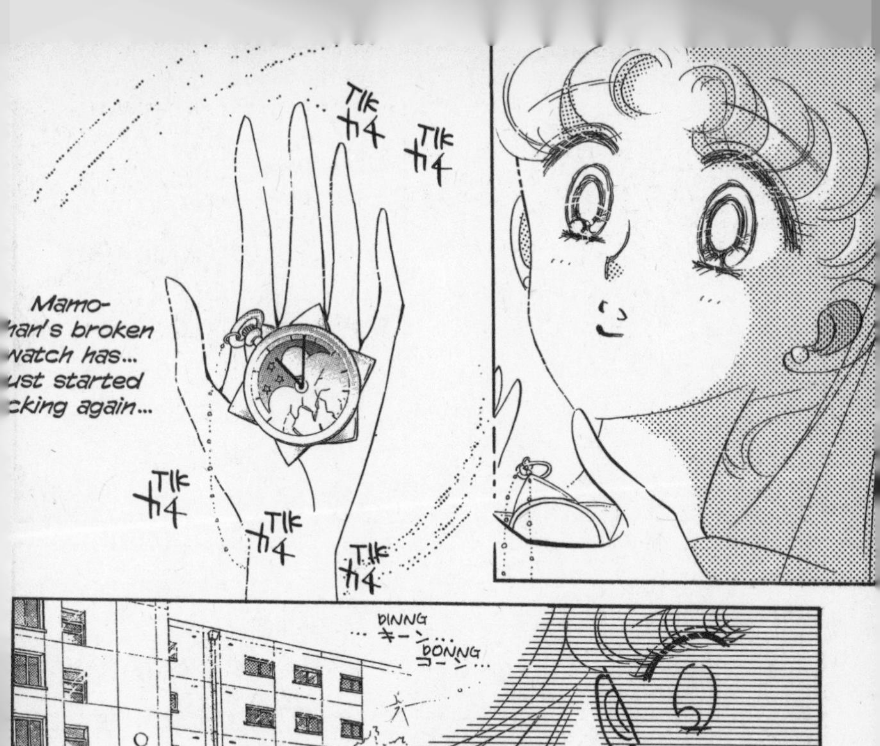
Mamo-
han's broken
watch has...
ust started
cking again...
TIK
TIK
TIK
TIK
TIK
DINNG
DONNG

Huh?
Furu-
chan...
...someone's
hanging out
in front of
the Game
Center...!
You
should
put the
moves on
Reika-
san...
Give
me a
break,
will ya?

Do you work here?
Yes. Can I help you?
I have business with...
...this game center.
Huh ...?
Oh, you mean you want the job?
PART-TIME HELP WANTED
UNTRAINED, OKAY. FLEXIBLE HOURS. GET DETAILS FROM THE MANAGER.
CROWN GAME CENTER
PHONE: 0090-3451
MANAGER: MOTOKI FURUHATA
You're the guy my uncle sent?
I'm Motoki Furuhata.
I'm the son of the building owner, and he's loaning me out as a part-time worker here.
Nice to meet you. What's your name?
Are you a college stu-dent?
Um... You're...
Let's see...
Haven't I seen you with Usagi-chan before?
I know I've seen you some-where.

..."Usagi"...
CHARING-LING
チャリラリラー
Endo...
Sorry, but could you go on in ahead of me?
Okay.
VEEEEN
PYUUN PYUUN
GLEEM
SHUU
...
FFT
GLEEM
From now on...
...I'm your good friend, Endo. Nice to meet you.
SHUU

CROWN GAME CENTER
ピューン PYUUN
ピューン PYUUN
チャリラリラー CHARING-LING
Furuhata-kun! You here? You left something in the club room.
ヴィーン VEEEEN
Reika-san!
Oh, you're new, huh? And good looking too! ♡ What's his name?
What are you talking about?
This is my good friend, Endo!
Endo ...
... kun?
するっ SLIP
バサッ THUDD
Ah!
An Introduction to Gems and Crystals Varieties Uses
The Green Kingfisher Stone: Jade
Green Column Stone: Beryl
What? You're interested in rocks, Endo-kun?
Reika-san knows all about that stuff.

You're staring.
You like jade?
Jade is two different rocks. Jadeite is a pyroxene, and Nephrite is a tremolite.
They call Jadeite the "true jade" and it comes in various shades.
And Nephrite has a deep green.
The pink spodumene rock is called Kunzite. The color is pale and beautiful, don't you think?
And the purple-blue stone is Tanzanite, also called Blue Zoisite.
Oh, I'm sorry! I just keep on blabbering, don't I?
No...
As it turns out, those very same four stones...
...are stones that I have...
DINNG ...キーン
DONNG コーン
DINNG ..カーン
コーン DONNG

Hey, it's only because we have a mission meeting tonight!
るんっるる
DA-DUM!
Today's the very first time I've ever gotten to go to your place, Ami-chan! ♡
I'm so happy! ♡
Veeee-chan! ♡ Sorry to keep you waiting!
Usagi-chan, I get embarrassed when you call me V-chan!
Ehh? But that's the name that suits you best!
HIKAWA SHRINE
Rei-chan! ♡

I'll be there soon.
There's a dark shadow on the flames of the burning sun.
It is a bad omen.
Exactly as my predictions said.
What did you try to predict?
What's to come.
And the results were not fortui-tous.
Does that mean ...
...that in the coming battle we...
...will be fighting with a handicap?
...I don't know.

Wooow! ☆ Ami-chan, you live in an incredible condominium!
No, Usagi, they call something this incredible, Condo-millions!
Amazing!
'Cause it takes millions to buy one.
Mako-chan, you know. everything!
Wonderful marble entrance way!
V-chan, make sure you don't drop that sword!
TRIPP
AH!
KANK
Ahhh !!
AWWWW!
V-chan chipped the marble!!
It isn't my fault!
A-Ami-chaaaan!
Forgive me!!
You're a lot more careless than I imagined.
It's okay! Don't worry!
Marble is pretty soft, so it's damaged pretty easily.
And I was just thinking of talking to you about that stone sword.

This is diamond, said to be the hardest substance known to man.
V-chan try hitting it against the sword.
SHUNNK
KONK
KACHANK
As you saw...
...the thing called the world's hardest substance broke to pieces...
...That sword isn't any ordinary stone.
AWWWW!
Ami-chaaaan!
Your diamond! Your diamond!
Don't worry! My mother has more of those than she knows what to do with.
I asked Luna to investigate the sword and some fragments of the temple on the moon.
Both are made of extremely strong elements that have never been seen on Earth.
Perhaps I should say...it hardened into what it is now.

Also, there is a strong toxicity to them.
...When Usagi...
...When the princess stabbed her-self in the previous life...
...We were bathed for an instant in light. That's all I remember.
Is that when it hardened...
...into that odd toxic rock?
...The Moon Castle on Mare Serenitatis...
...was, at one time, a beautiful crystal palace. Our kingdom...
...The moon, long ago, didn't look so lonely and dark.
It was more white...
...and shining...
...Did the enemy...
...change it into a planet of death?

HEE くすっ
TEE くす HEE くす
Oh, Usagi-chan! She always goes straight to sleep when the talk goes technical.
すぅっ zzz
There's also her worries about Tuxedo Mask.
She also met her mother in a previous life, the queen...
She's got a lot going on.
I'll bet she's just exhausted from the stress.
Quietly, quietly...
zzz
パタン KACHAK
We...
...ended up not hearing how to seal up the enemy. The most important part.

A sacred, legendary sword to protect the princess...?
So even if we find their main base...
...and come face-to-face with them...
I have this heavy, cursed sword... How do I use it?
How are we supposed to defeat and seal this enemy away?

PLIP
…ポタッ
I remembered...
I was rescued... by Tuxedo Mask...
...by Mamo-chan...
I was in Mamo-chan's bed...
...and I woke up then... just like now.
From his apartment...
...I saw a sunset just like this...
...I'd love to play a game right now.
The Sailor V game.
I want the relief it brings.
SNIFF
くすん
SNEAK
そーっ
CROWN GAME CENTER
CRO

How strange...
It's like I'm being drawn here...
CROWN
...Also strange...
B-BMP
...that my heart is racing like this.
B-BMP
Is it because I...
...saw that guy...?
There's somebody over there...
...in front of the Sailor V game...
VEEEEEN
Yo, Usagi-chan.
...Eh...?!

...Mamoru...
...You are...
...Chiba?!
どくん B-BMP
...No way...
...Usagi-chan?
Sailor Moon...
SST
She's a bun-head just like you are. Maybe it's just in fashion.

...Mamo...
...chan...?!
Usagi-chan, this guy just started working here. My good friend, Endo.
I'm a first-year student at Furuhata's school, K.O. university.
My name's Endo.
...A good friend of "Big Bro" Furu-chan?!
A college student?!
...That means he isn't...
...Mamo-chan?
B-BMP
But...
...Nice to meet you.
His voice... His looks...

Even the warmth of his hand is...
...exactly the same...
It's like he's right here...
...before my eyes!
I hear you're good at the Sailor V game.
Could you teach me how it's played? I was hoping to see you, so I could ask.
B-BMP
...His smile...is a little cold.
!
PEEP
PEEP
Mina!
Somebody...
...is clearing Sailor V game levels at an alarming rate...

We're going to the game center!
...Who could it be?!
AH!
Usagi-chan?
CROWN

!!
There...
...with Usagi-chan...
Mamoru Chiba?!

Tuxedo Mask!!
...What is *he* doing here?!
I mean... He's supposed to have been taken prisoner by the Dark Kingdom, right?
He's the guy who bumped into us this morning...!
It couldn't actually be Tuxedo Mask! Mamoru Chiba?!
No...
Look at his eyes...
He isn't quite what he seems... I've got a bad pre-monition.
It's best to keep Usagi-chan away...!
Away from him!
DINNG キーン
DONNG コーン

Usagi! ♡ Let's go home together, okay? ♡
Sorry! I can't today...
Humph! ☆ What's up with Usagi these days? ☆
Usagi-san is going back and forth to the game center these days. It seems she's infatuated with a new worker there. ☆
HMPH! ☆
Usagi-chan!
You're going to the game center every day, right?
...He isn't Mamoru Chiba, you know...!
Usagi-chan!
...I know...
...all that.
...Furu-hata...
PYUUN
SHUPIN
SHUPIN
This game is really fun.
You can clear level after level, and the next new level appears. It goes on forever.

It's as if the actual Sailor V is fighting.
No...
Maybe it's more accurate to say ...
...that somebody somewhere is on the other side of the console ...
... forcing her to fight.
ピューン PYUUN ピューン PYUUN
ウィーン.. VEEEEN
Yo.
Usagi-chan. I've been waiting for you.
You're as skilled as I thought.
I am not... Endo-san, you're much better ...
ピューン PYUUN ピューン PYUUN
It's like you are one with V, and you know all there is to know about her.
ドキン B-BMP
Yes, that's right.
...ドキン B-BMP
...She's a very strong ally.
ピューン PYUUN ピューン PYUUN
...
You sound as if you've actually met her.
シュピーン SHUPIIN

To tell the truth, I've seen her my-self.
Really?!
She was very cool.
...ドキン B-BMP
...right. She's a much more reliable ally...
ドキン B-BMP
...than I could ever be.
Than Sailor Moon could ever be?
...ドキン B-BMP...
Eh?!
Your hair style...
...makes you seem very much like Sailor Moon.
Tell me, where do Sailor Moon or Sailor V usually spend their time?
Is there some secret command center?
...ドキン B-BMP
...I have to...
...go home now...
ドキ B-BMP

Usagi-chan!
Come again to-morrow, all right?
I want to learn...
...more of your secrets...
...Usagi-chan!
B-BMP
Good...
...bye.
B-BMP
...My suggestion doesn't work on her...?!
B-BMP
B-BMP
B-BMP
...What'll I do?
Those cold eyes could make me faint...
...Like they could seduce me.

...I can't refuse... It's like I'm ready to spill all my secrets!
I mean, he looks so much like him!
Come on, "Usako."
Call me that...
Not Usagi, "Usako"...
They're together again?!
Come on, Furuhata-kun!
When did you make yourself such a great-looking friend?
You've been hiding him, haven't you?
M-Mako-chan! Mako-chan!
What's with Ms. Versace here?!
...Um...
You wouldn't be "Big Bro" Furu-chan's... acquaintance could you?
Not a chance, right?
Do you know those two guys?

Yes... Oh ...?
My name is Reika. ♡
I go to the same school as Furuhata-kun.
But that "close friend," Endo, I don't know. I've never seen him before.
There was an Endo-kun who was Furuhata-kun's friend, but...
...he was a more weak-type guy.
He's a coke-bottle glasses, otaku type.
But I haven't seen him lately.
They must've become friends recently, right? Furuhata-kun and that Endo guy.
But nobody at school seems to know where this Endo came from.
It's dangerous to let him play the Sailor V game any more than he already has.
He's investigating us. I know it!
...If he...
...actually is Tuxedo Mask... Mamoru Chiba in the flesh...
...we can't make any false moves.

I'll be in there soon!
The command center...
Heh heh heh...
!
Hold it!
The two of you are in cahoots.
What are you trying to do to Usagi?
What are you plotting?!
GLEEM
CROWN GAME CENTER
CRO WN

Mako-chan! What's the matter?!
Why'd you call us to the command center all of a sudden?
Usagi! I've been waiting for you!
You are forbidden to go near him!
He's the enemy! He was after the Princess from the start!
...By "him"... You mean Endo-san?
B-BMP
Don't go deciding that he's the enemy before...
He's the enemy! What would you do...if he were able to steal the "Legendary Silver Crystal"...?!
But, I've got it on me like always.
Why the sudden concern for it?
VEET
VEET
!!
What ?!
An intruder ?!

WHOOSH
VEET
No! Nobody but us should be able to enter the control room!
VEET
KAKK
WHUDD
Mako-chan ?!
One step closer, and she would have had it.
Humph! Useless!

Tuxedo Mask!
I never guessed that the control room would be directly beneath the Sailor V game. The strong shield kept me from sensing it.
No...
It isn't true, is it?!
I'm glad I could hypnotize her so quickly ...
...then it was easy to get her to guide me down here.
Transform, everybody !!

Venus Power: Make up!!
WHOOSH
Hand over the "Legendary Silver Crystal!"
EYAAH!!
DAKK
Sailor V Kick!
Take this love whip and wake up!

Venus Love-Me Chain!!
BZZT BZZT BZZT BZZT
VRSH
PATCH
VWAA
BWAA
...He's too strong! He'll destroy the whole command center!
BCCHT BCCHT

SHAA
WT
BZZZT
Venus!!
KANK
GLEEM
FWAAA
Finally! The "Legendary Silver Crystal!"
Heh heh... Now I have it!
Dammit!!
Kh...
Usagi! Transform! Fight!
You have to get it back! The "Legendary Silver Crystal!"
...Why is Tuxedo Mask...
...fighting with Venus?
Usagi-chan, what are you waiting for?! You have to fight now!

...Fight?!
Fight Tuxedo Mask?!
Heh heh! Ah ha ha ha!
Am I having some kind of nightmare?
Or is this actually happening?
Didn't they take him to be a prisoner of the Dark Kingdom?
Usagi-chan! Snap out of it! Don't be deceived!!
He's a fake Tuxedo Mask!
WHOOSH
GAMPH

VOOSH
What do you think you're doing?! Out of my way!!
VWATCH
KRAKK
KRAKK
Luna?!
Luna?!
No...! Hang in there, Luna!!

He is not Tuxedo Mask!
Moon Prism Power... Make up!!
Luna, open your eyes!
Luna ....!!
POHH
!

The "Legendary Silver Crystal" is...
POHH
Usagi-chan! Now! Use the stick on Luna and Mako-chan!
Moon Healing Escalation!!
SUUU
TWITCH
...Hahh...
Mm...!
I cannot forgive this...!
False Tuxedo Mask...!
If you think you can seduce me with a handsome smile, you're badly mistaken!

In the
ame of the
Moon!
The one
playing pranks
will be punished
by me, Sailor
Moon!
PAAAA

VCCH
VCCH
VCCH

...Who...
...is that woman...?!

Heh heh heh... Well done, Tuxedo Mask!

With the "Legendary Silver Crystal" in hand...
...I have no use left for you!
And you, Sailor Guardians, this will be your grave!
Who do you think you are?!

Heh heh... Princess.
No matter how many times I meet you, you're always a bratty little child.
Don't you remember my face?
It's true, though... I am not like I used to be.
That woman...
She's...!
...I am, Princess Beryl!
Queen of the Dark Kingdom!!
Princess Serenity!
I believe your true wish is to die at the hand of Prince Endymion!
Ha ha!

...Prince Endymion?!
No...!
It can't be true?! Are you really...
...Mamo-chan?!
•to be continued•

Pretty Guardian Sailor Moon Early Concept Art Exhibition!

Five Sailor Guardians Early Concept Art Costume Suggestions

Usagi Tsukino - Sailor Moon Concept Art

Preview of the First Installment in the Series
(Published in Nakayoshi, 1992)

ranslation Notes

panese is a tricky language for most Westerners, and translation is often more art an science. For your edification and reading pleasure, here are notes on some of e places where we could have gone in a different direction with our translation the work, or where a Japanese cultural reference is used.

ige 19 & 20, Usako and Mamo-chan

ese are two examples of how nicknames can be made from one's name in Japanese. Although Usagi d Mamoru are both single-word names (meaning that normally these names would not be broken up), th Usagi and Mamoru break up the syllables in the name to make their own unique nicknames for the ier.

Page 82, Tokyo Tower

From its construction in 1958 to the present, this landmark has been a symbol of Tokyo and an ever-popular tourist attraction. It was originally built as a tower for sending out analog terrestrial broadcast signals for television and radio. At the time the Sailor Moon books were originally published, digital television was still in its early planning stages, and the Tokyo Tower was Tokyo's main broadcast tower. Since the advent of digital television, it turns out that Tokyo Tower is not tall enough to provide Tokyo with consistent digital transmission, and so the new Tokyo Sky Tree has been constructed to replace Tokyo Tower's broadcast duties. Tokyo Tower still remains a vital tourist destination.

ige 156, Moon Bunny

noted in the translation notes for Volume 1, Usagi ikino's name in Japanese name order is a homophone Rabbit of the Moon. Thus Makoto's finding a real "tsuki usagi" makes for a bad pun. (As mentioned in the note Volume 1, rabbits are as associated with the moon in oan as "little green men" are with Mars in the U.S. and ier western nations.)

PART-TIME HELP WANTED
UNTRAINED, OKAY. FLEXIBLE HOURS. GET DETAILS FROM THE MANAGER.
CROWN GAME CENTER
PHONE: 0090-3451
MANAGER: MOTOKI FURUHATA

Page 195, Crown Game Center

Just a warning. Don't try to call the phone number. There's an extra zero in there and four missing four digits. In other words, it's a fake phone number much like the 555 phone numbers used in American movies and TV shows.

Page 197, Green Column Stone & Green Kingfisher Stone

These are literal translations of the kanji found in the Japanese names of the stones. Beryl often crystallizes in the shape of a long hexagonal column, and I would assume the kanji for jade is because the stone is the same color of green found in the plumage of the bird, kingfisher.

Page 201, Condo-millions

This is an approximation of an Japanese pun. Large, multi-story condominiums and up-scale apartments are called "mansions" in Japan. But the Japanese have a word man which means "ten-thousand," and another word oku which means "hundred-million." The author did a play on the word "mansion," calling very expensive condos oku-sions. An oku of yen is worth about a million dollars.

Page 209, K.O. University

The very top universities in Japan are mostly public schools, but two are private universities, Keio and Waseda. As the reader might notice, K.O. sounds a lot like the Japanese pronunciation of Keio. The fact that Furuhata goes to K.O. University is a sign of his high intelligence and prospects for a very successful career once he graduates.

Preview of *Sailor Moon 3*

We're pleased to present you a preview from *Sailor Moon 3*. Please check our website (www.kodanshacomics.com) to see when this volume will be available in English. For now, you'll have to make do with Japanese!

——暗黒の王国 ダーク・キングダムの女王 このクイン・ベリルの手先になって
あたしから「幻の銀水晶」をうばうために——きたの!?

うそよ! こっちを見て! タキシード仮面!
まもちゃん!?
うさぎちゃん おちつくのよ!

彼は 一時的に あやつられてる だけよ
クイン・ベリルを たおせば……!
プリンセス おまえの知る 王子は もういない
死んだ王子の体に 「幻の銀水晶」 の力を ふきこんだようだが ムダだ 死んだのだ
王子 エンディミオンは わが おおいなる 支配者 クイン・メタリアの 力で 甦ったのだ!
この わたしと おなじように 力を授かり
ダーク・ キングダム 最強の 戦士として!
「死んだ」!?
ダーク・ キングダムの 戦士として よみがえった!?

うそよ!
!!
強い!!
くそおっ
ジュピター　だめ!
これ以上　応戦したら
司令室が……!!
……うっ
!!

Pretty Guardian Sailor Moon volume 2 is a work of fiction. Names, characters, places, and incidents are the products of the author's imagination or are used fictitiously. Any resemblance to actual events, locales, or persons, living or dead, is entirely coincidental.

A Kodansha Comics Trade Paperback Original.

Published in the United States by Kodansha Comics, an imprint of Kodansha USA Publishing, LLC, New York.

Publication rights for this English edition arranged through Kodansha Ltd, Tokyo.

First published in Japan in 2003 by Kodansha Ltd., Tokyo, as *Bishoujosenshi Sailor Moon Shinsoban*, volume 2.

ISBN 978-1-935-42975-3

Printed in Canada.

www.kodanshacomics.com

9 8 7 6 5 4 3

Translator/Adapter: William Flanagan
Lettering: Jennifer Skarupa

TOMARE!

STOP

You're going the wrong way!

Manga is a completely different type of reading experience.

To start at the beginning, Go to the end!

That's right! Authentic manga is read the traditional Japanese way—from right to left, exactly the opposite of how American books are read. It's easy to follow: Just go to the other end of the book and read each page—and each panel—from right side to left side, starting at the top right. Now you're experiencing manga as it was meant to be!